Bathhouse and Other Tanka

Bathhouse and Other Tanka

TATSUHIKO ISHII

Translated from the Japanese
by Hiroaki Sato

A New Directions Paperbook Original

Some of these translations first appeared in earlier versions in the following publications: *Partings at Dawn: An Anthology of Japanese Gay Literature*, ed. Stephen D. Miller (Gay Sunshine Press, 1996); *Snow in a Silver Bowl: A Quest for the World of Yūgen* by Hiroaki Sato (Red Moon Press, 2013); *Poetry Kanto* (2014); *Common Knowledge* (January 2015); *Ribbons* (2017); *Tokyo Poetry Journal* (Winter 2020); *The Green Integer Review* (January–February 2022); and *Washington Square Review* (Fall 2023).

Manufactured in the United States of America
First published as a New Directions Paperbook (NDP1581) in 2023

Library of Congress Cataloging-in-Publication Data
Names: Ishii, Tatsuhiko, 1952– author. | Sato, Hiroaki, 1942– translator.
Title: Bathhouse and other tanka / Tatsuhiko Ishii; translated by Hiroaki Sato.
Description: First edition. | New York, NY : New Directions Publishing Corporation, 2023. | "A New Directions paperbook original."
Identifiers: LCCN 2023016479 | ISBN 9780811231343 (paperback)
Subjects: LCSH: Ishii, Tatsuhiko, 1952—Translations into English. | Waka—Translations into English. | LCGFT: Tanka.
Classification: LCC PL871.5.S557 B38 2023 | DDC 895.61/6—dc23/eng/20230503
LC record available at https://lccn.loc.gov/2023016479

10 9 8 7 6 5 4 3 2 1

New Directions Books are published for James Laughlin
by New Directions Publishing Corporation
80 Eighth Avenue, New York 10011

ndbooks.com

CONTENTS

III

PREFACE

The tanka poet Ishii Tatsuhiko believes that his medium, the 5-7-5-7-7-syllable verse, is a one-line poem. He also believes that this verse form makes it as modern poetry properly when it is constructed as part of a sequence.

Ishii is not alone in the belief that the tanka is a monolinear verse. Practically all contemporary Japanese poets regard the verse as such—contrary to the general assumption, outside Japan, that the five syllabic units that make up the form indicate it is a cinquain. Perhaps inspired by this, Adelaide Crapsey devised an intricate five-line form out of the tanka to write her delicate poems.

This is not to say that the tanka has been fixed as a monostich since it came into being (probably) in the seventh century. Although it has been written down as a one-liner where the space allowed it, there is no question that the 31-syllable tanka, "short song"—also called *waka*, "Japanese song," or, as Arthur Waley simply called it, *uta*—had, from the outset, the tendency to break up into the upper hemistich of 5-7-5 syllables and the lower hemistich of 7-7. This spawned the sequential form of renga, "linked verse," that alternate the two hemistiches up to one hundred times. As is well known, the renga's opening verse, the hokku, became an independent verse, which is now called haiku.

The tendency to write tanka down in one line whenever space allowed it—except when the verse was presented for aesthetic appreciations—became standard after the modern printing method was adopted in Japan in the mid-nineteenth century.

Not all tanka poets have since treated the tanka as a monolinear form. Early in the twentieth century Ishikawa Takuboku (1886–1912) wrote tanka in three lines (while also writing one-liners). (In *Poems to Eat*, Carl Sesar translated Takuboku's tanka *back* in five lines, as it were.) Miyazawa Kenji (1896–1933) wrote tanka in one to six lines. [See *A Future of Ice: Poems and Stories of a Japanese Buddhist* by Miyazawa Kenji, tr. Hiroaki Sato (North Point Press,

1989).] More recently, Hayashi Amari (b. 1963) insists on a two-line format. They are exceptions nonetheless.

In creating his single-line tanka, Ishii usually writes in such a way as to annihilate the 5- and 7-syllabic units even as he sticks to the 31 total syllables of each line. You may ask: How does Ishii count the syllables of the foreign phrases that he often incorporates in the original languages in his tanka—Latin, English, German, Greek, Sanskrit? The answer: They are counted according to Japanese pronunciation. For example, "I shall be too late," the White Rabbit mutters to himself as *Alice's Adventures in Wonderland* begins, comes out to 11 syllables when read as *ai sharu bii tsū reito*, rather than the 5 counted in English.

Finally, most Japanese poets in this genre employ no punctuation or symbols, although the folklorist and tanka poet Shaku Chōkū (Orikuchi Shinobu: 1887–1953), for one, famously employed punctuation, especially in interpreting classical uta. Ishii does, too, at times abundantly. These features, including variations in dash length throughout the poems, I have tried to recreate in the translation.

For further historical analysis of tanka, its lineation, and English translation, see my "Lineation of Tanka in English Translation" (*Monumenta Nipponica*, Vol. 42, No. 3, Autumn 1987); "Forms Transformed: Japanese Verse in English Translation" (*Mānoa: A Pacific Journal of International Writing*, Vol. 11, No. 2, 1999, and Frank Stewart, ed., *The Poem Behind the Poem: Translating Asian Poetry*, Copper Canyon Press, 2003); the introduction to my translation, *Cat Town* by Sakutarō Hagiwara (New York Review Books, 2014), and my collection of essays *On Haiku* (New Directions, 2018).

Ishii Tatsuhiko has published eleven books of tanka, from his collection *Rowan Tree* (Nanakamado) that appeared in 1982 to *Passing Daybreak Rows of Cedar Trees* (Akebono sugi no namiki wo sugite) in 2020. In this book Japanese names are given the Asian way, surname first, except for the names of the poet and translator on its cover.

—HIROAKI SATO

I

THE VOID OF THE SEA

For Mishima Yukio's soul

> In this garden there's nothing. I've ended up coming where no memory or nothing else exists, Honda thought.
>
> —Mishima Yukio, *The Decay of the Angel*

Tolling the knell of the bell (of lamentation) over the sea. . . . The day the writer left, already distant

I shall pray to the God of an alien land. ——Saying . . . *Requiem aeternam dona eis, Domine*

> The night of the day Mishima Yukio died, I wrote a poem for the first time, something like a fourteener calling out to the one newly dead. . . . Soon that poem-like thing quietly went on to contract into a classical verse form. Into an ancient verse form called *tanka*!

It was a brown night. Yes, when I called out intimately to the dead one who had just died. . . .

The boundary separating the dead one from me appeared to blur gradually.

It was the dead one (not to be off guard with) who suddenly grabbed the boy's heart.

The problem was the succession of words spun out toward the dead one,

and only writing them down and rereading them seemed the solution.

Formless and vacant words!
      But soon they too were molded into a (forgotten)

poetic form.
      The words became a song.
            Well, then, let me sing.
                  ——That was the Day of Wrath!

Dies irae, dies illa. . . . Ah! From, beyond the River of Oblivion, a
   voice comes ringing

Enshrine in wrath the one who killed himself in wrath, under the
   moon. Even in awe

not forgetful of the (violent) panting of the dead peering into the
   bedroom window. Soon enough. . . .

At the Rite of Blood Food (those yet to die) surround. The sacri-
   fices for the wrathful dead

Keening over them in spring and weeping for them in autumn is a
   later courtesy, still, dreading the dead. . . .

The snow I dreamed of was ebony-black. It fell in pure-white darkness,
   say that, if you want to

> When he read my youthful tanka, Nakai Hideo observed: Here's a
> tanka poet like a young warrior Mishima Yukio might have sent over
> from the Netherworld. . . . A tanka poet like a young warrior whose
> refreshing, lithe body throbs under his armor of scarlet braids!

Confutatis maledictis. . . . when I intone, waves, slightly, rise in my body

The accursed, but who? In evening calm on the inlet a sailboat, has, no hint of men. . . .

His talent as inexhaustible as the sea, they said, of him, that misfortune, the depth of, it

At dusk (by the sea!) anemones abloom the boy writes poems, his, habit to be alone

In the depths of sea fog a voice of God, ——Sing! so He orders. A new song

God's voice falsetto? In the beginning, the Word was with God, or so it was said. . . .

Must have been a boy (or, at most a youth)! When He created the heaven and the earth, God,

A treasure from the sea. For example, a beardless poet's head on a harp

Casting up a fragment of something lost. . . . It is too cruel. What we call the sea

I knew rushing billows have numerous voices. Just about when I was bored with sailing

Walking the beach on horseback gallantly a young warrior. Sailors long for him I hear

In the heart of one yearning for the ocean sea (before long) salt begins, to, crystallize. . . .

The oars broken the sail torn, still, shall I offer praise. To my leader
Stella Maris. . . .

> But that young warrior has now reached middle age without achieving
> any worthy exploits. —Mr. Mishima, you wouldn't recognize me from
> thirty years ago; I've gotten fat and these days I often sweat. The sweat
> even smells of sulfur, endlessly. . . .

Lacrimosa dies illa. . . . As if to match my singing voice the sea,
again, howls

Lachrymose day, they say. That many geniuses die young I (of no
talent) lament

Had I at least the ability to kill myself. . . . In the rain the moorings
remain untied (in any way!)

I might be soothed by the sound of waves, even encouraged.
Though my mind is still lax

The boy writes poems, the youth wants a body of stone. In the
storm of the night

Don't say (ah) *that youth* (ah) *lasts forever* (ah! I hear it now, the
sound of waves, of time)

Once that poet (at a cape) declared. That, *only gray hair and wrinkles
wait for us*

Suppurating sea of pestilence, slowly swelling, it, urges a (certain)
decision on the youth

Lightning way beyond. A poet without a so-called hometown, one,
might say, and yet. . . .

It was daybreak (at seagulls' calls) (closing (quietly) the book I was reading) I knew

This ringing sound of a bell of which temple? Morning meditation, someone's repenting his sin

Shall I be ashamed that I've lived longer than the dead? Though the time isn't the time for us

The mists let up, the universe clears up, and still my heart does not rejoice in the prime of life

> Nakai should have suspected that the young warrior you discovered was counterfeit. Like the protagonist of Mishima's last tale named Tōru. . . . No, under the armor of scarlet braids there may have been nothing from the outset. Like the garden of Gesshū Temple under the summer sun, the garden compared to a sea on the face of the moon!

I hear a faint echo of the sound of waves—— *Libera me, Domine, de morte aeterna. . . .*

To (rather) yearn and pray for eternal death, allow me. My wristwatch (this morning) stopped. . . .

Time to unravel, its tangle, I'm somewhat tempted to believe. Karma (and, my) transmigration

What I'd finally never have. Wife, and children, and a body resembling a shield of steel

The rope that links the past of regret to the future, what? Before dawn (look!) the sail's full

J'attendrai ton retour. . . . No, the day of wrath, to meet in the court
of judgment, that's what I wish

Say the eternity of heaven and earth is an error if you want. *My life
has come later than yours*

Comparing human life with dew this mooniness (moon, drops
into the sea!) laugh if you laugh

Deception at five p.m. The sailboat the midday moon has tugged
away, is no more

Symptomatic future's decline. "See, depends on each heart" is such
a cruel word

Only time flows eternally——. On the moon's surface there is a sea,
that's such a beautiful lie

What exists is bound to perish. Both the sea before our eyes, and
the writer's final book. . . .

Well then, I'll sing.
    Of the grief of waves.
                Of the void of the sea (of each)
                    And of its fertility!

HIDING BEHIND A CLOUD
Elegy for Genji the Shining Prince

TRANSLATOR'S NOTE:

"Hiding behind a cloud" (*kumo-gakure*) is a metaphor for someone exalted passing away. It is the name of a book (*jō*) in *The Tale of Genji* that exists only as a title in some lists, prompting some to assume its content was lost. Of the fifty-four books that make up the *Tale*, it is placed after the fortieth book, "Maboroshi," and before the forty-first, "Nioi-no-miya," as the romance has been handed down over the centuries. Eight years pass between the fortieth and forty-first books and Genji's death is intimated in the interim.

Among those who have imagined what the "missing" content might have described is Marguerite Yourcenar. In *Le dernier amour du prince Genghi*, included in a collection of her short stories, *Nouvelles orientales*, she attempted to fill the blank by opening it in this way, here translated by Alberto Manguel with Yourcenar: "When Genji the Resplendent, the greatest seducer ever to have astounded Asia, reached his fiftieth year, he realized that the time had come to begin his death."

Ishii's sequence "Hiding Behind a Cloud" is based on the threefold inspiration he had during his trip to New York City at the end of 2001. The trip's purpose was to see operas at the Metropolitan Opera House, but 9/11 had occurred just a few months earlier. So the morning after his arrival in New York he visited the ruins of the World Trade Center's twin towers. One of the operas he saw was by Richard Strauss with Hugo von Hofmannsthal's libretto, *Die Frau ohne Schatten* (The Woman Without a Shadow), a new production directed by Herbert Wernicke and conducted by Christian Thielemann.

On this trip Ishii had brought with him the six-volume Iwanami paperback edition of *The Tale of Genji*, to him the single greatest work of Japanese literature. The sequence he composed, "Hiding Behind the Clouds," consists of fifty-four tanka.

Ash on an old man's sleeve
Is all the ash the burnt roses leave.
Dust in the air suspended
Marks the place where a story ended.
—T. S. Eliot, "Little Gidding"

A thousand years! The world unable to inherit someone to follow
your noble shadow, has, continued. . . .

Although words thrive, ah, everything is totally different from his *Tale*!

> You who were a dead person a thousand years ago, you who were such
> an impeccable being as to be exalted as a figure to be raised as a deity in
> the sky, I cannot help deeply mourning you now, a thousand years later.
> Since you hid your noble shining self in a vacant book only with its
> name, we have continued to endure the nonexistence of an impeccable
> being for as many as a thousand years.

I sorrow over his heart deep in amorous attachments. Of what a
man ought to be (a human ought to be). . . .

The hibiscus curtain is warm but flowers do not bloom this spring
evening, so someone, comes to, tell

Remorseful that he has loved way too many people the man's, his,
excess flesh

The standing hollyhock noisily scatters. You should deal (always)
coolly with the Lady

There ought to be a flower blooms in winter as well. Indulgent love
(on each occasion) with just one

Plucked a wild rose just because he wanted to. . . . Ah, the man who
   has both power and beauty

The man's cold treatment. He's gained an incomparable rank, or, so
   I, only, heard. . . .

Isolde and her Lord, man and the Lady, that, I hate <and> separating
   the two!

The sin she broods over unbeknownst, what? They are the two lives
   that never meld in the end

At the close of the world where dew has come to bond no more
   (still!) this heart of hateful weariness

Rather than the next world this life. Let my floating name flow as I
   do (often) on heartfelt things

Ought to be different from the usual so he instructs. His last action, this!

Cold and colder this planet. Death resembling life and (life being
   equal to death)

> I'm singing this elegy in the giant city destroyed by the hateful violence
> resulting from an accumulation of intolerances. This city had cheer-
> fully recognized itself as the capital of the world for the last hundred
> years, but now it has turned into a city of requiems lamenting both the
> several thousands who perished and the view that was lost.

Smoke and dust erupt in the watch towers. No matter how many
   centuries pass man is history's slave

The tall towers collapsed, and the war. . . . In this world that's turbulent
   enough without them

Both landscape and human life will be lost in the end, I know they
will but even so. . . .

Memories of loving a landscape being more intimate (than! memories
of loving a human). . . .

The tall towers that are beautiful (*were* beautiful!) I visited again,
saw, and wept.

Count on a magician and look at the blue sky! The snow-white
towers as they form

Mankind hadn't even been reformed. Ever lecherous, ever bellicose!

As one who remains alive I'll (continue to) live. *Ruler and subjects
look at one another*

everyone wets his clothes with tears. Though cursed as a fellow good
at getting on in the world

Is that a crime? To, live disheartened in the world where only trou-
blesome despicable things multiply

Simply living for love ought to be praised. Ah, the men fond of
battles that are repugnant

Both parents and children and siblings (actually) live in a battle-
field. Though the winter sky is cerulean

That which was once beauty. . . . A soldier by himself in the ruins
burns a single rose

Can we in the end find a being of your impeccability only in a tale? For a thousand years since you hid your light mankind has continued to be an imperfect being committing only foolish acts, even though, having said that, I hesitate to call you, the impeccable being, a happy man.

Human life is strife. Yessir, strife! Even at the close of the evening when life is about to end

Out in the field ——*O weh, Falke, o weh!* So aggrieved was, the young emperor

Wo kommt sie her? The execution ground for the sin called love is in the heart

Forgotten even by your lovers you die, that's all. In a winter when the snow doesn't fall

Everyone thinks of someone alive. Rather than a human in the next room (just about) to die

Humans are all blind. The sin called love, you violate even mother, in the darkness of night

Calling mother's son younger brother is natural. Even though she said that shouldn't be out. . . .

A winter rose has brittlely scattered. Reflect on it, it's the life he didn't know himself

Lost as foam fades away. . . . The sound of a bell at dawn and, the life of an enemy in love

Sin in an afterlife will be light, even saying that (he's a man, you know!) is close to a curse

All the time (mother) terrifies! When I hear about the precedents of Theban Kings

The baron left old and useless. Yes, he always had some resemblance to my mother-in-law. . . .

Charles Swann, mort! so he says and falls obstinately silent. That is, has Shining, hidden?

> In the opera I saw in this city, the deathless woman, the elf queen who was like the light itself, was trying to become a human who must die, for love. To become a human who must die means to have a shadow. A human is a human because she has a shadow. And you, who were the incarnation of light, surely had a shadow. It is you like that I deeply mourn a thousand years apart, in a city vivid with the scars of mankind's foolish acts.

The magicians going back and forth in the big sky (there were two planes, I hear) had no shadows

In the city of silence a great many posters ——Ah! where in the world is the princess?

To look at your body, that wish. . . . I reaffirm. In the ruins a thousand years afterward

Write them into tales, into poems. . . . Mankind's stupid acts (that never stop repeating themselves)

Good luck is inherited by children and grandchildren (*slowly slowly the gong and drum*), no, it doesn't, no

Suspicious of the ashes of roses on one sleeve. Youthful death better than to grow old and die, better?

Gloaming light it is. Though I call "a loser" you who hid yourself
behind the clouds

what remains is only the shadows. Yes, that's the way it should be, I
ought, to, nod in assent

That there's no lore of death I sorrow. The blank white pages go on
into the future into eternity. . . .

Schatten zu werfen, beide erwählt! If that is the way it must be

The ruins overflow with sunlight. . . . Ah, what's this? All humans
have shadows

This regret will never end, so, I think but. . . . *Il était grand temps.* . . .
you can, say that, too

Will be purified, and forgotten. The dead today all when a thousand
years (!) have passed. . . .

THE NIGHT ALL MANKIND GREW OLD

> The unmentionable odour of death
> Offends the September night.
> —W. H. Auden, *September 1, 1939*

Open (quickly) all the windows you have! Look, to witness the
sky-coursing evil intent

The day I climbed the tower. Yes, think of it now that day, I forgot
something important. . . .

Was there ever or wasn't there a tribe (autumn sky a perfect lapis
lazuli!) without a foolish act

I drop a wine cup (of glass)—— I dare ask. Did whatever took place
take, place?

The ocean plane shines in the sun. . . . From now on every place will
be a battlefield, sure

The gong for setting sail! A luxurious cruise ship (and, an extremely
elegant aircraft carrier)

The world spotlessly cloudless. . . . His eyes clear • what an evil •
martyr • was he?

To mankind (angel falls from heaven is fate. If he doesn't) I'll have
nothing to show

How difficult all this. In the middle of the journey of our life, to
call only dogs dogs

Even I (Ah, the Holy Mother and Child) wasn't born because someone wanted me to, or, so....

From today on we are also orphans. Floating on the reservoir the sail of our ship indigo

There was a man, listen, Dwelt by a churchyard.... (The story of a boy with a wooden leg)

Ah, if only, we understood each other better! The midday of the city of disaster is our night

In the dive drunk customers discourse on the offence. On this clear September night

I thought of those September massacres.... This, a line of a poem too bitter, to recite

Another star shoots! Over the field where horses tired of marching hang their heads low

Mankind's is a history of mistakes. That may be the only truth, when I reflect on it

Midnight when battlefields and the world keep silent, who's that? The one who heard the scream

Airports and the future shut down. You see, this, the night all mankind grows old at once

Would I were a boy again! Ah, since then I've listened every night, to Gould's Bach

Everything and all, collapse and fall! At midnight when mankind's
afraid quietly——

September, 2001

AT THE FOOT OF POPOCATÉPETL

Giving up on everything I've come here   both my closest friends
and my motherland on tiptoe

The slight bit of honor I'd hope for   abandoning even that as I
stand at the foot of the volcano

I will dedicate a spurt of blood   to this mountain that's been
spitting out fire since ancient times

Or rather I'll dedicate poetry   weaving together my thoughts
coiling up in my heart

What is it that the snotty world has endowed me with?   me this
weak-kneed being

Avalanches of greens as far as I can see   this country once the
Kingdom of the Sun

Street-corner fairs are flourishing this morning too   with tourists
as customers just looking

From town to town chapel bells ring and ring   toward morning
a young man passed away

A vendor by the street his smile his cracked fingernails   as I'm
about to buy a piece of earthenware

A fragment of damask handed down since ancient times?   No a
remnant of the glory of a king removed

A late morning fair in a winter resort!   A tattooed sluggard indo-
     lently whiles his time away

Knowing very well it's bric-a-brac I buy a necklace   from a village
     girl with limpid eyes

An image of innumerable fingers spinning threads rises   from a
     single shawl of silk

I'd purchase along with the vendor   the shoddy fabric the native
     wears on his body

The old man is a renowned craftsman   he pickpockets souls from
     tourists from foreign lands

A central plaza on a clear day   a *terrorist* goes blending himself in
     the crowds of people

The holy hall built with the stones from a pyramid that they'd collapsed
     itself collapsing almost

How many daredevils are there?   among the young men idling in
     the ruins

There in that backyard that's an erratic boulder   we too are erratic
     children left by this age

Serfs at the very end of the royal lineage?   those who laid manure
     in the field of hegemon trees

The fallacy that it is a race that excels in strength over wisdom
     right under the blue sky

In the riverbed placer gold hides   the down-and-out prince in the
    hubbub of the town

Let us read while weeping   the letter of cruel forgiveness to the
    heir of the kingdom destroyed

The young man's blood that spurts out   as an offering to the
    benighted and idiotic God

The memory of the slaughter has faded   as I pick pebbles along
    the bank of a darkening stream

The bondage that can't be cut   that ties the human beings to the
    earth filled with filth

Decorate the funeral procession with the flowers right here   'cause
    the graveyard is so faraway

For the old and dead the wormwood   for the young and dead the
    buttercups that know not time

The scratchy sweetness of the candy the caravan has carried for me
    all the way I love   weeping

The difference I ask the ruler   between to be killed in battle and
    to be killed as sacrifice

I approve the seller of his country   yeah I'd known for long the
    storm toward the offing would come

Both shattered gold and King's secret treasures have been utterly
    robbed   by the iron-clad knight

Was entrusted with a company   Stop the refugees surging into
     the border cities

Ruby-like blood clots   on the Indio soldier's upper arms that are
     pitilessly emaciated

They did not know love   neither the conquistadors who swarmed
     in from the sea nor the half-naked kings

I hum a poem by a fallen soldier   while scowling at the world
     with a great many demands

The stagnant atmosphere of the evening dusk   as I nibble at a
     fruit shriveled up sweet dried in the sun

A distant ancestor born noble   bought an aboriginal prince and
     turned him into a slave

A twinge of guilt as I drink taking a bird's-eye-view of the lives of
     the lowly   from Tippler's terrace

Summer on the plateau slow to dark   Isn't there a means of turn-
     ing a sorrow into a joy?

A symptom of a fiery mountain spurting fire   the youth with a
     thick breast doesn't hesitate to die for his lord

Overflowing with dogs and those who perform magic   the mar-
     ket in the evening darkness

In the tiny windows of shanties lights begin to turn on   from the
     sky stars start falling down

Thou shan't talk about black or white!   Asleep under the eaves a
    vagrant mestizo boy

Hummingbird's azure feather pinned on his collar   this evening
    alone the spoiled kid is a prince

A shooting star almost skims a treetop   loving each other a man
    and a woman with red skin

The lover is a soccer player   he should kick degenerating mankind
    even if he dies for it

A night train that's dashing away like a streak of light   carrying
    soldiers and refugees

Everyone be poor is the revelation   from heaven above the precipice
    that rises high

I forget the friends of olden times   clashes never ending the
    world has already completely darkened

THE NIGHT I SLEPT WITH MY FATHER

1

Just arrived Black Incense, fragrant. The night I slept with my own
     father turning cold quietly

Caution! No sooner or later, the Ides of March is coming, the settle-
     ment of solitary souls will press on us

I'll die without showing to my closest friend.   His hair and miniature
     painting in his locket

I close my exclusive anthology. Having grown up as a child who
     might not have been father's child

Death comes suddenly. A purple wild thistle bloomed all of a sudden
     this morning I've heard

The vacuity of the high noon light. The rebellious army's fort
     (without a trace!) has rotted away

Crying all alone is that someone's child? Rough for a while the
     storm has deserted the wild field

Escape this real world at once! If you can't remain as innocent as
     you are as a human being

Will be with a flash of light. On the day when my own body, ceases
     to be my own body

When I think back he was my father with whom I contended——,
     only the stars flood the sky

A dark gray midnight! Even my scarce sincerity has plunged into an indefinite labor strike

Rapping me on the shoulder mysteriously——. My father wrapped in a lacquer-black woolen cape

2

My (dark) heart wearied even of reading books alone I (quietly) listen. To distant thunder

I furtively observed in the starlight. My inviolate father's breathing (at the brink of death) asleep

The prophet's eyes glittering like Ares and (pity!) the poet's pale tongue

Where a meteor fell oh yes here's where on this isle there's the grave of the emperor removed

I prick up my old decrepit (still working) ears for the musical sounds (celestial bodies play)

Subtle premonitions of a natural calamity. In the sky I look up a shooting star the color of fire

You should kill him yourself! Father, the youngest child clear with hegemon's signs in his eyes

The night storm (at once) has passed into a sky full of stars. The place I'm from now like a dream

We are soaked with flooding stars. Having survived (barely) the age
   of plagues

Weren't they ominous? The words the son (hurriedly) pours into
   his own father's ear

I divine the tomorrow of this star by a star (receding into the distance).
   Listening to a Messiaen

Beauty perishes and only death flourishes——. I having wandered
   into a forest of stars ever lucid

3

The mind that thinks the movements of stars that draw arcs are
   useless is despicable I say

The tents holding on to the skid row along the river, darken into a
   turtle-dove colored dusk

Going to a war buddy's funeral in ceremonial dress uniform. A single
   lily in his hand

To die at the peak of your life. That's what's permitted only to young
   men, I tell you

Give up the ace in the hole. For both gambler and poet to die (at
   the height of their lives) is an honor

We pick up casings. For us it's fate to live a momentary life and die
   (with no attachments)

Won't that come to me? The tomorrow when I'll be called a *résistant* that died nameless

My (youthful) uncle wasted his life——. The arrow spiteful time shoots has black fletching, I hear

The battle situation isn't to our favor. The brand-new (comical) drummer was (shot and) dead

Soaked wet and decomposing wreaths before the gravestone. Slaughter all the politicians

Dagger hidden he sets out on a journey. ——Even in youth's daylight there's an eclipse is what I mean

He has a young hawk's eyes, they say——. The one who confronts fate and battles with time

4

The climax was the summer of my twenty! To reflect so is too simple. In the evening dusk of our life

In what way to kill father. Under the sky utterly clear, at the three-forked junction of youth

Burned the (treasured) books of uncle of useless death. In the floor fireplace of our old house to be removed

The rose garden also went wild——. Drunk and befuddled night after night (my) cheeks turned ugly blue

The sole son becomes a tyrant——. If his father were a sagacious
    ruler, even more so

The ancestral land also declines the poet even discards the poem
    that's written so! With his poetic soul

I once pleaded with father. To let me go to war with myself as myself

Childless and growing old all myself. It's been a long time since the
    Rite of Blood ended

This flower resembles you——, so saying my heart's friend, picked.
    A lavender violet

Making me yourself also a mistake. The fury at father that revives
    every morning

The mirror that shows me growing more like father is dark. In the
    clarity between snowfalls

The enemy called father who's in the distance. Was a man with a
    bullet mark in his upper arm

5

Whom in the next world to leave a message. Thou shan't transmit
    Brutal King's private evil

In the blue sky a cloud as if brushed with a brush stroke. Those who
    write poetry are all liars I know

Sun darkens. The youngest son who's grown old inherits none of
father's weaknesses

I put a single camellia in a vase. Intently counting up my father's
retaliations

I'll pour unto younger brother's grave. A cup of blood-colored
(slightly bitter) excellent wine

Finished memorizing? The thinness of the reddish earlobe I bite of
younger brother who's dying

When where and how did I lose. The wristwatch I'd stolen from my
father

The king if grown old is abolished. The heir who has survived is
abandoned (on the final day!)

Was my father who detested poetry (in secret) reading? The collec-
tion of my youthful poetry

Shall be slandered. That, I as a solitary poet died without writing
father's funereal homage

Would that poetry were a grave! Under the moon, the forgotten
grave at the end of a field of wild weeds

The poet who sees with an eagle eye and stings with a sharp snake
tongue——. His heart burnt raw

6

Younger brother, whom Hypnos is to compete with father and defeat. Carelessly asleep

One summer day all clear——. Younger brother (pity!) as if he were the sheep's first kid

A wind blows. The summer sun's rays somewhat cool the funeral procession departs at eleven a.m.

The one who's beautifully born passes away fast. At times before the flowers bloom

The scene for the murder was wasteland. The sun was too blinding someone said

Where was the family tree messed up? Younger brother ran through the blood that ran through father

A harvest not reflected on. The pigeon-chested older brother quietly bows his head

Younger brother's pride is younger brother's shame. The shame the older brother avenges with blood

Eternal summer is solely younger brother's. Father raped him and older brother killed him

Let's bury younger brother. In the diary with Moroccan leather the color of congealed blood

Sin crouching at the gate. However blood-soaked yet innocently fresh older brother's sin

Lying by younger brother's corpse, older brother weeps. In the tent in the shadow of a laurel tree

7

Time (accompanying) the runner in a soaked shirt leaves behind him in the evening dusk

Jealous (after all) of younger brother who maintains his youth in poetry, older brother

Wearing a rubber-coated raincoat with its collar turned up the assassin hides a dagger in his hand

After killing a streetwalker the knight in a plague doctor's mask is swallowed up by the ground

Pointing to the city to solve a mystery the young warrior gallops to the right of the three-forked junction

Add sin to sin. So, cries out to me from the ground younger brother's bloody voice

The scar chiseled on the wanderer older brother's brow. The grassland is vernal no matter what

Shall I buy the man with a workman's apron and carve God's words in his upper arm

Eternally young younger brother. ——As the lookout for his older brother now decrepit and wheezing

A tuft of younger brother's hair——. Hidden at the bottom of a box
never to allow father to touch it

Even releasing my own blood will be after I write poems worthy to
be left for the next generation

Time with a lacquer-black mane eats up——. All those things that
are alive

8

In morning cold I've embraced. The unlicensed prostitute with a
boyish breast and girly hips

I deprive the master of his brand-new servant. As a chip for a card
game

As an officer's duty he trains the year's fresh products soldiers doing
suicide drills

Blond hair and blue eyes. The young emperor gathers together only
slaves with those

Immorality sprouting in his clear eyes. ——The boy pricks some-
thing on the settings block

He tickles his orderly's innocent spine with the tip of his saber——.
On emergency night duty

You shan't stare. At the young unspoiled man asleep naked in the
shadow of a palm tree

Men with nothing but their own bodies——. The battles continue
encompassing many centuries

Now to determine as adopted heir. The boy servant that pushes his
old decrepit master at will

I've bitten my younger brother's ibis-colored nipple. Nipples exist
for love and lust

I point at the vast sky with a thumb! Since I gamboled with a
whimsical and vulgar boy

More unfaithful than prostitutes are boys I've learned. ——At a
glimpse on a night bright with stars

9

On the last night we are men who all sell our lovers (for thirty
pieces of silver)

At the sword tip a fatal dose of love. Mad-feigning younger brother
superior to older brother though young

The imprisoned poet's youth——. His dream: the killing of all the
successors of the king

Streetlights turn on. This evening too boys are lightly rouged (to
sell fresh greens)

I look up at the starry sky. At the (invisible) starry sky lamenting
my unluck in an abandoned garden

Cut if you want to cut. The clove-shaped wick tip of the flame of love you've stirred yourself

Toss a single gory ball a beautiful pearl! Into the cup of the crime of the regicidal king

I try to read a will in starlight. A deeply suggestive " [blank] " between the quotation marks

The following day older brother's widow weds. The uncle being an usurper in any age

The new emperor's bloody edict. ——A poet who has written truth shall be put to waist cutting

The rest is silence——. The messenger who brings the news of father's death is lean and all black-clad

The remaining days are (as it were) *palimpsest*. With your own blood if you are to leave your poetry in writing

10

Older brother confining himself in a library where dark is slow to fall——. Vainly surviving

The oracle states, ——Solitary traveler, be cautious! At the three-forked junction of death and life

Public holiday raining cats and dogs——. That day a dragon tattoo was on younger brother's back

Allusion to what? The scar chiseled on the forehead of the one who's being driven away

Who is it that's leading the blind king by the hand? Amidst the stormy wild northerly wind

Is this my death costume? The black coat damaged during pilgrimage travels

That's the way it should be. Thanatos holds under his thumb the ending of a life of wandering

I listen to the War Sonatas alone. The breast pain that has continued since having younger brother precede me

The wound he had in the days while a newborn wrapped in soft cloth hurts. Now again

throw into the lapis lazuli sea. The youth who remains asleep rolled up in coarse cloth

With younger brother's corpse before him older brother, ——wants father's heart, so he wept

Thou art spring! In my photograph album I seal my younger brother up (as a spring pupa)

11

Because the actor for the statement who announces the ending of this star is (still!) a boy

To the film actor who killed the uncle just the other day today I
   allot the role of a parricide

By God I shall not write a threnody for father or an elegy for
   younger brother——. So I pledged but

you shan't talk about bravery. Because it's after you were defeated in
   a battle for the beloved for the moment

Do you have an alibi? On the day my father died I was in a house of
   ill repute in Rome

They encounter at the three-forked junction. The funeral procession
   of the ill-fated youth and that of his father

The unceasing indigo-gray rain——. All the fruits on the family
   tree rotted and dropped

Tell the goddesses of vengeance the Erinyes, ——that. Unexpectedly
   I may have killed my father

The evening dusk of my heart of bleak blizzards. Love (in the end)
   holds murderous intent

A civil war may be turned into an epic. An in-house struggle in a
   clan into a (sour) ballad

The good news a white-crowned servant brings to tell is the news
   of death. ——From the Underworld

The reverberations of the collapsing Galaxy——. Today yes this day
   shall deliver, and, destroy me

12

Thunder God, has boomed——. In my heart there's me (all alone)
cursing Heaven and Earth

Let me be struck by lightning. In the Inferno, arrogantly as (cruel
brave general) Capaneus

I've covered in black gauze. The (ancient and stern) *portrait* of
father in the uniform for battle

Behold with a brand-new mind! Drawing an infinity symbol ∞ in
the sky. An eastern buzzard

Shall I walk on with a profound regret in mind——. Through the
world of aerial perspective

A lone winter traveler with his color fading cast in the depths of my
heart an evening rainbow

From the window close to Heaven starlight enters. To the epitaph
on the grave on the floor of the church

I dissolve the pledge made via the dark eyes of father and son——.
With my own blood

In a revolution the poet died and left his epic unfinished——. I've
burned the manuscript

I dare preach *monarchomachia*——. The heavily wounded prince
peers into the king's funerary box

I'll mix a clutch of father's ashes with that of younger brother and
scatter them. ——In the wasteland

A monocle on the table, shines. The night I slept with my own
   father decaying quickly

ORESTES IN HIS OLD AGE

ὦ τέκνον τέκνον,
οἴκτιρε τὴν τεκοῦσαν
—Sophokles, *Elektra*

Rappelons-nous que chez les Anciens il n'était pas d'autel plus sacré, entouré d'une vénération, d'une superstition plus profondes, gage de plus de grandeur et de gloire pour la terre qui les possédait et les avait chèrement disputés, que le tombeau d'Œdipe à Colone et que le tombeau d'Oreste à Sparte, cet Oreste que les Furies avaient poursuivi jusqu'aux pieds d'Apollon même et d'Athênê en disant : «Nous chassons loin des autels le fils parricide.»

—Marcel Proust, final paragraph of "Sentiments filiaux d'un parricide," deleted against the author's will by the editorial department of *Le Figaro* at the time of its first appearance

Appearing to enjoy having nothing to do by his warm hearthside. . . . but, the King

has a heart he's unable to clear up. Both the hero in his youth (and the great ruler now)

a continuation of sleepless nights and restless days. . . . Such was his life!

The smell of blood of the past, rises. So does from the cup of wine I quaff this evening again

Those days it rained all the time, it, seems. . . . when I passed my voice-changing period

Everyone wanders. Even if the one who'd grown up in a blessed household, the boy. . . .

That's the way it is, besides. . . . Domestic violence, yes, you see! Cruelty, yes, you see!

The puberty that hardly grows. Especially if the mama was the (in truth) enemy. . . .

It isn't that a battlefield is not limited to a hill where shells fall (yeah!) I'm saying

He must kill! somebody. . . . on the very border where the boy turns from puberty to youth

Either to kill mother in the twilight (or, to kill father in the broad daylight) . . . if there's no other way

Even if you became blind that'd be too late! The king slaughterer also killed his sleep I hear

The remaining scent of a daybreak dream. Embraced by mother of the past and groaning

—*the rest is silence.* So mumbled the prince, his mother, her death, as it was

A dream of a sinking ship. . . . Waking from a dream Agrippina becoming violently furious

Until I was called a young man I had yearned for being one dreaming about being one. . . .

As for mother you see, it's a child's wish to meet her again. If it weren't a wish, to kill her too

The legends of mothers killed by their dearest children. Even if the sea calms in the twilight. . . .

Wiping the rim of the wine cup with my thumb, I then ask [the true meaning of a human's life]

Whoever it may be every child is a parricide! As long as it has dived through the birth canal (bloodied). . . .

Revere the mothers whose delivery scraped their lives off or made them lose their lives, children!

So many months and years since then. . . . In the port how many times did the ship burn?

Powerless as years accumulate. . . . even the color of the ocean seems as if ink has been poured into it

Although acting cheerfully he's lost his own flower and his flower seen by others, meaninglessly. . . .

Growing old is more painful than death. Furthermore, if everyone were a parricide. . . .

Illusion of the human world, that too. . . . The exploit in your prime, that, yes! The reputation, that, yes!

Just about the time lights turn on in the houses the King must grow old all alone

Even the moon from the sea is dark. When yet another friend has preceded you pronto

Probably it isn't too late, I tell you. He unties the rope and quickly (look!) a wind rises

What stars! Just because an old decrepit parricide has rowed out in the sea all by himself

The gladness of aiming for the island when old. . . . The island where (that!) dear fair-skinned aunt resides

I don't mind someone singing of us. Whisperingly ——that, the sea has closed over them

For the punishment for killing his mother once upon a time he dies much older than she. Tell them, that

I'd stay in mother's womb! Though going by boat pains my old body and the world is dark

One hundred generations of human life are just one night. Out of the gray haven, to the blessed island——

AN ANNOUNCEMENT TO MANKIND

The Sea Rises and Boils . . . the Earth Quakes

> À peine ont-ils mis le pied dans la ville en pleurant la mort de leur bienfaiteur, qu'ils sentent la terre trembler sous leurs pas; la mer s'élève en bouillonnant dans le port, et brise les vaisseaux qui sont à l'ancre. Des tourbillons de flammes et de cendres couvrent les rues et les places publiques; les maisons s'écroulent, les toits sont renversés sur les fondements, et les fondements se dispersent; trente mille habitants de tout âge et de tout sexe sont écrasés sous des ruines. . . .
>
> —Voltaire, *Candide ou l'Optimisme*

With, a dark gray voice, I'll tell you.   ——That, in a second, so many humans, died

To destroy mankind. . . . well, that's simple, see.   The earth (a little bit) shifts, is all

To modestly (moderately) live, and die like worms.   While you utter, Ohhh gee!

He was sitting at the gate of the city, but there was a voice. . . . . Quoth   ——Sodom destroys (itself)

Seemed like a victor. 'Cause, you know!   Humans beaten by a rain of fire and running away

On this star there's no, falsity. There, is, only   a species intently heading to destruction

If we are to die let's die together! Right, that, you know.   I just say, in, mankind's twilight

Even you, are, aware of this!   What we truly ought to fear (yes!)
  is mankind

Has mankind (yet) destroyed itself?   The sea rises and roils. The
  earth shakes. Without cease

And so, I announce to mankind.   ——Do die away! Along with
  merciless God

Days of Rains of Fire, Continue

> Seitdem das Pulver erfunden ist, kampieren die Engel nicht mehr.
> —Friedrich Schiller, *Die Verschwörung des Fiesco zu Genua*

Days of rains of fire, continue. . . . .   Everywhere in the world,
  continue. Rains of flames of fire

Yes (may I too) say this?   ——That, it's been a world of wars and
  disorders, since, we were born

The river divides, just about here. . . . Roars of guns were (for a
  while) continuing. Thunderously

NO SOULS CAME FROM HIROSHIMA U KNOW. . . . Upon hearing
  that I nod. In my dark heart

Was a ferocious fire. So much so that your soul would burn up
  (before you had the time to say   oh!)

A scandal, let's call it that. Today too the news (again) comes "Our
  battle results were glorious. . . ."

Do not forget! The fact that the soldiers, were, (too) young, and, emaciated

In the battlefield there are no angels.   ...... Though there may be (soldiers') dead souls suffocating in gun smoke

Can, (I too) say quietly? —*I am the enemy you killed, my friend*

Head wave, doesn't rise. . . .   In human history. . . . the rain of fire that poured into my town too

Landscape with No Human Beings

> *Haikunterke Haikoshitemturi*
> *Moshiresani kamuiesani tapkashike*
> *chiehorari okayash*
> —Chironnup yaieyukar, "Haikunterke Haikoshitemturi"

Of a landscape. . . . can you (really) sing? Though you are a descendant on the victorious side

(Even the landscape) was all robbed from the (indigenous) race. That, and, this

The landscape is, that is, God, there was a (rough and innocent) age, once, upon, a time that, said, that

(The one-eyed) wild God (from the cape) turns to look back⟶ at mankind (grappling each other)

Shoot an arrow at landscape! If it, may, be, that, there is God (that is destroying itself)

Over (the landscape) a rain of fire ceaselessly falling. . . . Deracinate
   all! Mankind

At the edge of slaughter how beautiful the evening sun—— ('Cause)
   the river is as red (as that!)

With my eyes used to disasters (in the monitor) I look. At the
   landscape with no human beings

God is dead and. . . . humans disappear. . . . the landscape, remains.
   With a godlike sourness

Moon   at heaven's center!   You, should, love, the landscape
   without anything like humans

II

TO THE TANKA POET
Upon hearing the news of Tsukamoto Kunio's death

> Oh Barbara
> Il pleut sans cesse sur Brest
> Comme il pleuvait avant
> Mais ce n'est plus pareil et tout est abîmé
> C'est une pluie de deuil terrible et désolée
>> —Jacques Prévert, *Barbara*

We once upon a time. . . . So he began and stopped, the tanka poet
who lived all alone

The pantheon that was built on youth's ambitions too. . . . Behold!
There's no one there any more

> Tsukamoto Kunio and Okai Takashi revolutionized the traditional
> poetic form of tanka in the second half of the twentieth century—
> during the hardship and empty prosperity that followed Japan's defeat
> in the Second World War. Yet, with Tsukamoto, I felt a vague scorn when
> I read his work for the first time: If these tanka of his are highly thought
> of, mine, too, should be appreciated. . . . I had just begun writing tanka.
> It was his seventh collection, *Seisanzu*, and I'd bought it because of its
> resplendent binding.

The boy in a faded memory picked up the book in his hands, the
early summer's, indigo

What shall I write in my diary . . . . Turbulence the day before yesterday?
The evening glow of poetry?

Discard in the dark green waste land! hatred (and the notebook all
filled with hackneyed tanka)

The hollyhock has collapsed at last. You don't need to know anything like love to write tanka

He releases thunderous words like God. The tanka poet in summer clothes

Whom is the tanka poet to fight? Striking him down with a cypress fan. . . . assailing him with his powerful memory. . . .

The heat of that summer! End of the world? people wondered, so, I heard

A triumphant avant-garde tanka poet? Men, feebly, from their hearts, are crumbling. . . .

In between fights you look up at the stars. . . . Wow, how few they've become!

To know a man, see, a man. . . . On his nakedness, the moonlight, falls like words

Wash a horse, and then, play. . . . The études of twelve compositions, from the first piece

The regionally limited poetic form isn't infertile either. If there we a poet of blue blood

The rowan red to the end! The custom be that the blessings are sprinkled with vinegar

The defeat at the end of a reckless war provoked a rejection of many aspects of Japanese culture. The ancient set form of tanka, for one, will face death, some feared. It was then that Tsukamoto Kunio dashingly emerged like a savior—with a body of pieces that combined surrealism and aestheticism, an attractive Biblical flavor and odd erudition. Termed avant-garde tanka, his work provoked at once fierce condemnation and intense admirations.

The youth's wilderness is indigo. . . . The dream in his prime (Look!) is dyed of madder

Shaved your beard the first time? He asks a poet who's popped up, out of an older man's considerations

Relying on food called poetry to live. . . . Confused by the lover's (unexpected) wedding

Throwing into the whirlpools of mankind's unfathomable desire. Poetry's fetus and its rose

Has the flower burnt out? Now, (poetry) is, in an Ice Age, are, you saying that?

Yeah right, depends on how you put it. Just as you kneel before an angel, kneel before a dog too!

Clear bright autumn sky, elegant luminous moonlight. . . . Though this world's full of epigones

An old man's wits, shallow, this world, rumbunctious, warbling, bush warblers'. . . . fake voices

Its value, how much? In rainy Brest a violent fellow sells himself

Meteor shower, fierce! Writing tanka and discarding it the men part (for the rest of this life)

Strife at midday. I discuss the skylark with a youth who does, not, know, the least, bit, of poetry

Whoever put up with . . . this century of the suppression of (ah!) quietly darkening poetry

The night the first snow falls ceaselessly a fire faraway. . . . Pity, my fatherland is burning

> Tsukamoto perfected a unique style recreating the complicated style of the eighth imperial anthology *Shin-Kokin Wakashū* that was compiled during the period when the ruling class moved from gentry to samurai, it is said. As a result he spawned many an epigone. For the second half of his life, however, his own tanka endlessly imitated his own vainly singing of his loathing of war, some criticized. But it was during that period that his reputation solidified as a tanka poet.

False words a son who doesn't take a bride says (to his mother). . . . *mulier ecce filius tuus*

Not, just the blood! The calamities that the sobbing youth is to inherit from his father

Should be, forgiven. . . . That a son despises his stern father as intolerant

A model citizen he is, but I say. ——That, the one who strikes his father should be surely killed

The distancing voice of father! Not to be revealed even after his death, that certain secret

Do not turn your eyes away. From your fatherland in twilight, from the degradation of poetry

In the darkness, *Mais où sont les neiges d'antan?* . . . In a voice akin
to that of a raptorial bird

An exiled poet's (vacant) grave? To a terrifying degree, ivies, thrive. . . .

Words sticky throughout the mouth. ——I saw trouble in the distance,
the trouble of poetry

Bombardment extends even to the forest. Even to the forest of the
poet's darkening soul

Poet's eternal siesta. . . . Heaven Beings Fester in Five Phases. . . .
Poetry enfeebling. . . . I think, of

Poet's eternal siesta. . . .   lit in it a (faint) light . . . .   which, I love

Poetry. . . . harmful, a dream. Even the world, finally, due to poetry,
liquifies. . . .

> Tsukamoto's death in 2005 was lamented, as it should be, but why is it
> that we feel a king of cruelty? Is that because the difference was so great
> between his work in the first half of his life brimming with miraculous
> brilliance and his work in the second half full of painful void? The
> impression of the latter is so strong I can't help feeling that Japan's tanka
> world since his death has continued to be beaten by *une pluie de deuil
> terrible et désolée* in Jacques Prévert's song "Barbara" that he loved to sing.

The city of betrayal is wet with moldy rain and asleep. . . . Feign
enlightenment, you philistines

The rain's like boasting. . . . The tanka poet's high-pitched voice
returns echoing (from the past?)

À quoi bon, un duo? The gardener, asks. You see, both in Heaven, and on Earth, there is Sodom!

As rumor has it, God's unpreparedness.... He sent (poetry) out of the overthrow

Rhyme and rhythm are a ladder to Heaven. I, pass, by, an Archangel with rosy cheeks....

The set forms, are, dead, the report, should come. . . . to, the one struck down in the rain as well

Old man wit, shallow, in this world. . . . it only rains, the youth's gaze, dark, the world

The gardener, wrote stage directions. . . . Fearfully, fearfully. . . . *Le monde disparaît. Le rideau tombe*

Struck by the rain! After the death of poetry. . . . both the war-torn hill. . . . and the city of terror. . . .

At the end of mankind's dumb acts the sky sobs. . . . See, the whole world is in the rain!

Without a break, the rain, falls. . . . In dark gray evening is slow, to his waterlogged planet

We once designed (the world). . . . .Leaving these words the tanka poet passed away

I fling a copy of a tanka book, into the River of Oblivion. . . . as if to bury the world

HONEYBEE'S WINGBEAT
Ode to Okai Takashi

The honeybee's wingbeat is faint——. The rebellious poet too lived
    alone in the end

Don't follow the one who leaves. The pantheon of poetry's gone
    wild with no humans left

> Of the two revolutionaries in Japan's tanka world in the second half of
> the twentieth century, Okai Takashi, who was younger than Tsukamoto
> Kunio by a generation, died in 2020, at age 92. He, too, devoted his life
> heroically to poetry.

You were once, discarded by lute-verse-wine friends. The waterfall
    frozen in blue gray

Emotions swirling, yet keeping stubbornly silent, head down, you
    set out on a pilgrimage

Briny winds beat the tent. The *nationalist* having a siesta again,
    groans in a nightmare

The right-wing tree, the left-wing avalanche——. The eyeless nomad
    follows a trail by a cliff

A faint warp of a hypothesis. But your blue heart is not here now

Was there a year deep in happiness? you ask. Living in the house
    dailiness of utter silence

Having piled up wreaths of words for the world and receded, in
    daybreak darkness. The packhorse

The right-side collarbone aches. Tired out because of doing nothing and trying to sleep

Looking for flowers and seeds the poet walks alone. In the dark of a word-solving forest called a library

Aged and yet bearing the sorrow of being a father the poet violently pants

The dark morning mist coming up close to his library window, behold! With his eyes smoking purple

Like a lamb crouching down beside him——. This lackey writing down a dictation

Saffron, I think of. Writing down on an indigo sheet a volume to be handed down to his single son

Okai's life was full of *scandalous* actions. He had started out as a poet in the most traditional prewar tanka school Araragi and had attained a princely position in it, but he was called an avant-garde poet along with Tsukamoto Kunio for his ultramodern style imbued with nationalism even as he was an activist of the radical left. A physician, he headed the internal medicine department of a large hospital, and while in that position he *disappeared* with a young lover from both medicine and tanka, for five years. After reemerging in the tanka world, he approached the imperial household and became the instructor of tanka for the imperial family, a move that provoked harsh criticism from those who had once worked with him in the left.

Will he be able to return safe? Winked at by the fallen angels hanging out around the city gate

A torment since morning strikes the passenger on the run, the rain
    the night train's crystal window

Reject all the different views——. The more distant from city dust
    the more lucid literary thoughts

I absolutely need an enemy says the physician as a cloud of poetic
    thoughts rises at the tip of his shoulders

Thou shan't lament your empty bedroom, wife——. It's a custom
    for a poet to sleep (one night) in exile

Don't talk of a defeat——. You rushed up the spiral staircase of
    temptations, did you not

Placed on the table a genealogy of poetry and (a plate of) fish salad
    ——. A dinner for the starry night

Banished how many times? So asked in the midday of no human
    voice no human shadows

A request written with a left hand— . The master is always absent,
    but hale and healthy

A picture postcard not sent in travel, has popped out. From the
    inside pocket of his spring wear

In the patio in finch-hued rain stands a (wet) man——. The sere-
    nade he hums to himself

The road to the station is a starry path, and the royal line of poetry
    about to come to an end

Even his shadow having soon faded the internist is simply absorbed
    in reading Exodus

But Okai's literary accomplishments grew indisputable and harder to criticize year by year. He reconstructed the ancient set form of tanka with fresh devices, even starting "tanka readings," sharply different from the traditional "tanka recitations."

About the king who returned from exile the world (even now) talks of the betrayal of that summer

The revolutionary poet, returned alive——. A quick transformation is also what makes him excellent

This the only alternative idea. At the toast his respected friend (who can't drink) sings a hymn

In the suburbs the garden (of Ideas)——. Though not to deride the wanderer's destiny

A disturber of tough luck isn't he. Debating the dead he admires fulfils his life

The shallows (of verse and prose) he wades through. Singing a new song that resembles a scream

Talks of the loneliness of Jupiter, does not sing with the (glittering) words of Venus

Close the wooden door with your hand behind you. Boys, and girls, the sacrifices of songs for the Muses

The Empress and formerly the tuberculosis specialist——. The sky over the illusory Palace quickly clears

Don't tell me you no longer care for me. How to recite my poems I'll think about before tomorrow

The predawn darkness of great earth. The veins on the backs of my hands aren't decorations

An epistle referring to a painting in a basilica. Angels (probably) in heaven

At the hour of the deadline a dog barks afar——. Luckily, my wife is right here with me

> Okai's death cast a shadow for Japan's tanka world in the new century. As if he had sensed this, the binding of his last tanka collection, *Iron Honeybee (Tetsu no mitsubachi)*, was totally black.

The tower near completion is also pervaded with silence (only) the bells ringing

The scent of temple juniper fades at the hedge. In his purple-gray coat the principal doctor of poetry

The evening rainbow's softness——. Finally will the traveler live at ease outside this world

Thinking of the vacant throne from now on I tremble. Awaken from the dream of being driven out of this country

There was a man who said Late in my life I'll drop vinegar and the time has passed swiftly

The endless future of a posthumous manuscript left with red marks. On a dark night of boundlessness

The tears I was barely able to stop. With his silver hair (still) trembling close to my eyes

The day called today I have buried. Counting my compunctions
   one by one

Inexhaustible laments I exhaust. In my confused right hand an
   argument on poetics I'm reading

The absence that pains me again. I too would abandon my life (of
   which only shames are many)

Over the single line erased from my notebook I sob and cry. If I
   could live oblivious of poetry

Lost at a scoop of tears I plead with you. ——Rule still as a dead
   man

The honeybee's wingbeat is faint——. At all times I think of you the
   most I would say

CLIPPING MY PUBIC HAIR
WASHING A HORSE

> Wondering why pubic hair is where it grows I am clipping my glistening
> one at midnight
>
> —Okai Takashi

> If I wash a horse it's till its soul grows limpid; if I love someone it's with
> a mind to kill him
>
> —Tsukamoto Kunio

I've spent the day covered with dreary clouds doing nothing.
With an eloquent poet as a friend

Don't curse him, Hairy bastard!   A man called the robber of a
nation, that bastard

That is absolutely clear.   Who the real thing is, where real poetry
is

Above all first pour hot blood.   Into those packed and built into
the mound

Don't ask about the way I splutter and stammer.   Even worse,
don't call me a ne'er-do-well

They aren't delicate in dealing with them.   Young poets these
days, before the Muses

Liquefy our poetic souls in the melting pot.   Let's stop with this,
the alchemy of poetic thoughts

Nonchalantly turning out poems till at last I'm old.   As blue
     admirals keep dancing in late spring

Try to pluck the Gagaku koto.   To make even the coarse wild
     Eastern man into weeping

A small man's pounding heart.   You brat I was scolded just yesterday

Absolutely casual.   So not to be called a hussy I share my sincere
     heart

I think I'm a wreck myself.   Born human to become an insignif-
     icant poet

Crestfallen even the man of the times wept they say.   After having
     made all that racket

Don't lament over anything petty.   In revenge I shut the anthol-
     ogy with great force

I firmly declined.   The tête-à-tête talk to decide because of the
     love he loves

In short it's a love poem isn't it.   That's what a poet ought to write
     to attract respect

Pulling it in softly.   Like the hem of a crawler's skirt, the fond for
     a poem's ground

Slippery slick paper.   Though not to hoodwink me someone
     else's poem written there

Fretfully I waited.   For the day when red-flanked bluetails come
     down the mountains singing

A horse stepping back struggles.   Seeing before him his old master
    he's come across for no reason

I drink from a stream under chrysanthemums.   Under the clear
    moon, my beloved horse's mane waving

A prince has been born.   The news I hear alone, thunders in my
    underbelly

Night by night her bedchamber in disorder.   Who has combed
    her hair negligent unsightly while asleep

Thou shan't throw in a joke!   Again shaving his pubic hair to
    become a warrior alone

You've sneered just now haven't you?   One trifling word could
    inflame a terrorist

Reaping reaping the grim reaper's scythe.   Knowing from the
    outset yours will be a defeat, fight

His is a strappy move.   The reins in his right hand, in his pocket
    the Qur'an he's reading

He walked straight up to him and struck him down, say.   With
    an old umbrella with a thump under the moon

My heart throbs from time to time.   Looking at a man's arms and
    legs fluttering down on the ground

Shall I go into enemy ground after all, by land.   After I'm baptized
    in the twilight

I've rinsed my mouth with well water.   The attractive-looking
    lacquer-black horse has also cooled

At the peak of winter the poet also clipped his pubic hair.   So as to
    sally forth on horseback to die

ABOUT THE GLOVE, AND THE POCKETS
In a blank space of the photo album: *Le monde de Proust vu par Paul Nadar*

A single photograph. A single portrait photograph that Nadar, not the famous one but his son Paul Nadar, took on February 25, 1896. Frozen there is a pair of lovers. Seated on the right side as you face it is a plump middle-aged woman wearing loosely made checkered street clothes for the afternoon, hair done up at the top. Faintly smiling, she places her hands on her lap, only her left hand in a kid glove.

Pure love? If we could remain smiling like this only for eternity!

The memory of the tryst to be left (Life is like a maze you know)

Just a minute ago I think I heard again. . . . (that) beating of the wings of (cruel) time

It has begun, see, already. The evening twilight for the lovers sobbing rose color

In my left hand <love>!   Let us leave it in the glove until it grows dark

Standing next to the woman is a smallish man beginning to show his age but endowed with a splendid moustache and beard. A large bowtie tied around his standup collar, he shows a bit of a pocket watch where the lapels of his jacket meet. You can't see his left hand that is placed behind him, but you can also see only half of his right thumb, either, as he casually puts his hand in his jacket pocket.

Has it reached you? (My letter added to) the fan made of cherry-colored Japanese paper

This hesitation to call you an imprisoned woman. See, I'm the one caught

In evening dusk so beautiful (as to make you sad). . . . Those eyes of yours (looking into the distance)

A kiss with eyes, something so called exists (in this real world). . . .

Now is eternal now. <Love> hidden from the camera and put in a pocket

> The woman is a famous demimondaine. Rumor has it that she received an allowance of 10,000 francs every month from the wealthy American dentist Dr. Thomas Wiltberger Evans who kept her. Needless to say, the number of men who courted her was countless. In the salons she held in her gorgeous villa innumerable gentlemen and artists, including many of her lovers, gathered. This high-class courtesan of whom Manet painted some portraits, and whom Proust is said to have used as one of his models of Odette de Crécy, was a large, gorgeous flower that bloomed in the demimonde of Paris. And her name? Yes, she was called Méry Laurent.

Days when I sobbed quietly, no, I had no such days! Even when I decked myself with white camellias

The many love songs I hummed for many a <someone>. Yes, from flower to flower. . . .

Is it a flame of lust? That which we cannot pacify with words

The yearning to live in a corner of a life. Of the life of <someone>

If I am to flow away let me always smile. Hiding <love> deeply

The man is one of Méry Laurent's lovers. A middle-school English teacher until several years ago, he seems to be living on an annual pension of just about 2,500 francs. Gathering poets and artists in his home to talk and argue every Tuesday is one of his few luxuries. Yes, he is a poet. The twentieth century to come will no doubt begin with this man's poetry, with the whole world expressing the highest respects to him. He is none other than Stéphane Mallarmé.

Our twilight (in the wind you create with your fan) burns quietly. . . .

Do you not feel it? You! The fountain nymphs inhabit without even wearing chiffon

The kingdom starts here. I once wrote in a poem *Je tiens la reine!*

I will (suddenly rise and) dedicate this salutation. Yes, the words that fly about

And those words in my pocket. . . . (along with your right glove. . . .)

TEACHER'S TEACHER: *IL MIGLIOR FABBRO*
A letter (to be read aloud)

From the distant edge of the Orient I, an immature poet, salute you—you, who sleep a gruntled sleep in the shadows of cypresses on an isle in the offing where those alive cannot live, you, the lord of a tomb dyed in gloomy evening glow and silence. Blacksmith far superior to anyone else, has your anger against the world faded yet?

To the teacher's teacher! To the teachers' teacher, my first letter. . . .

Myself a versifier in a *forme fixe*! Come to think of it, ain't I behind the times after all?

I think of. . . . Yeah right, of, the (insoluble!) fury of the poet far ahead of the times (you!)

The green of the cypresses being so dark. . . . The island of death, is, that, the island of poets?

The noble (poet's) fury. Just when the evening glow enwraps the world in darkness——

You were the maestro of all modern poets, the father of the entire twentieth-century literature. The song of the drowned Phoenician shone better by your relentless editing, the style of the novelist with a special-large Martini glass was corrected by you. It was also you who redoubled the fame of an old poet of the wild swans and an ancient tower, and it was you who allowed a Jew with soap in his hip pocket to leave a brothel in a city at the mouth of a river for the world.

The cruelest month, writing, something like that too, may well be, in fact something barbaric

Throwing lilies as they are in bud in the strait of civilizations, that
    sort of thing

Thou shan't miss the songs of the beautiful Sirens either, they say
    . . . . . If you are a poet

The ocean all at once darkens (the only one (in the world) without
    wax put in his ears)

Arrogant one, be struck by thunder! Whether you are a genuine
    poet or a hegemon

> But when it comes to you! No luck! Thrown in an exposed cage, con-
> fined to a psychiatric hospital. . . . The ingrate world was too cold to
> you. In the end you were expelled from your fertile motherland, the
> citadel of Capitalism, and died as an exile in the city sinking in black
> stagnant water. Like the poet who died by the Black Sea two thousand
> years ago. . . . Worse, with almost no one understanding him. . . .

Guard dogs only bark! At the tower crumbling though of a shallow
    history

In the window of the bedroom awaiting the hero of pilgrimage a
    blue parrot, and, the, moon. . . .

Evacuate, from the accusation. The accusation, that you are a
    deranged Fascist poet

Thousands of poetic lines that vanished in the waves of remorse
    (and, the unrecoverable, time)

Thou shan't laugh! At the mad old man's catch that is too gigantic

You are right in your anger. If possible, leave it as is, do not suppress your anger please. Because your eternal fury seems to embolden the poets following you. . . .

You should fade away as an old man with green hair. . . . Pity, the poet ain't an immortal

That's what happens, see? At the time, there were a number of poetry collections that were, stillbirths

His crowing was done by Beatrice's hands. . . . After the poet's death

The teacher's teacher's poetry will (yes!) never fade from memory

Postscript says: ——I will pay respects, someday. To your grave on the isle in the evening glow

WISTERIAS IN THE WILD,
or A View of My Small Study

> The flower clusters of wisteria in the vase are short and do not
> reach the tatami
>
> The flower clusters of wisteria in the vase: one cluster droops on
> the books I stacked up
>
> The flower clusters of wisteria in the vase: the flowers droop as
> spring's about to end over my sickbed
>
> —Masaoka Shiki, *Songs from a Bamboo Village*

I close, the book I am reading. Feigning, to be, the wise man said to
have ibis-colored eyes

Stacked up on the desk and quiet books of poetry. . . . .Pregnant,
with, innumerable memories

The aquamarine sticky note is now old. . . . . just about on that
page the hero died!

The startling hardships of the dead one, I, enjoy to read it. . . . in
my leather easy chair

Predecessors' dreams left, their, accumulations, like, them. . . . . .
Red Rome, and, green Hellas

Giving birth to a poem that remains 2,000 years from now, that,
such (ah!), a terrifying dream, I had

The first book of poems I ever read. The shoe that Lucy lost (still!)
hasn't been found

Java, China, and lamped Japan. . . . . The boy following the girl has
gone beyond poetry

I've lost my steps. In a forest of books . . . ever since (mother) gave
   me a book of poems

Millions of volumes by the ancients are all, superior, to my books
   . . . . my small study, cold

A remnant of gun smoke? The air in my study a wee bit muddied. . . .
   I, inhale, it, deeply

It won't go away! The odor of time . . . . even if we light the candle
   with a scent of gardenia

Even reading books, resembles, a crime. . . . Mankind, all, having
   lost sight of the Correct Path

The reader is wordless. . . . On the other hand the voices of the dead
   rise every time I turn a page

The, news of battles . . . reach. Even to the room where (a man, who
   feigns to be) a good reader shuts himself

I can't stay still, no! When I think of someone who must have been,
   killed, just now

The curtains left closed. . . . I open the window cloth, violently,
   whose audience color has faded

From a height, light, pours. Even, into, the garden (left wild) after
   the proper funeral

Flowers (of a weed) tall in height . . . Even one, of those flowers, is
   far, from me

Just like someone accursed, a stray cat, slinks by. . . . pushing aside a
    growth of chameleon plants

In late spring, wisterias in the forest on the other shore should,
    bloom. Have they bloomed, this year too?

The talented lady of the past, writes: Those blooming pliantly long
    and deep are, lovely

Leaning on the pine each to her taste, yes! Wisteria flowers, deep in
    color, their clusters long

As in the past blooming on the mountain. . . . I saw with my
    deceased mother, once, wild, wisterias

I hear mother's voice. ——Open, the window will you? The forest is
    burning the color of mauve

Just like fire, just like smoke. . . . The wisteria flowers on the evergreen
    just like (mother's) shawl

The wisteria vines are far far beyond the treetop. . . . Oh (!) the girl's
    at the end of the world

I've felt, as though I'd never gotten back the one shoe I had lost. All
    these years, ever since

I close the velvet curtains. Those limping, fill the earth, saying,
    something, like that

There's no, vase for wisterias. In my small study, in the first place, I
    have no, life itself

I, again, open the book I was reading. . . . thinking of things like,
    scar tissue on my soul, sadly

With few means of meeting my love, like Fuji the High
Peak that is in Suruga, shall I continue to burn?

—*Man'yōshū*

The menfolk's (sacred) wordlessness . . . . Blended in them, may
well be, <<the god>>

Having shed both secular dirt and grime of making a livelihood the
menfolk are stark naked——

The man who is sitting face down (on the rim of the hot water tub).
Has, a ferocious, back

Their brawniness (at times) is lovely. The menfolk wouldn't even
look up at the mountain above

The mountain that all its people have adored, is that, what it is?
Soaring all in solitude. . . .

Is it, all right, to sing of it in the words of an alien land?——*rì jiàn
gū fēng shuǐ shàng fú.* That's it

Looking down upon a countless number of limited partings. . . .
Even then, an immovable mountain, is it?

Brother Jūrō, why is it that you do not respond?. . . . So, asks, the
voice, congealed. In his heart

The battle buddy, older brother? If so, weep. ——Sour: if I am killed
place my corpse with, yours

In a pine grove in the mountain outskirts, as if spitting blood, he
    said. ——That's where our enemy has settled

To clear Father, his soiled name. . . . Looked after by my son in a
    previous life, and, dying

Whoever he may be, the son is a patricide. . . . Looking up at the
    peak soaring black in the predawn dark

Raise, a sail, that is as snow-white as your snow-white heart! On a
    small boat of your fantasy

How crystal-clear the peak I turn to behold every day! The white
    snow that does not melt in eternity

The painter's errand boy's cheek a brush of paint as blue as the blue
    sky, just one stroke. . . .

The day the colors have faded after the years. . . . If you could repaint
    it! Someone's life as well

Who will make the sounds of waves? Behold! The landscape in
    front of you is supposed to, be, wordless

Bearing up the weight of silence. Both the mountain and the men-
    folk immersed in the hot bath. . . .

Having killed his father the boy goes on to resemble his father (his
    dark body, in particular!)

Decet timeri Caesarem. So told the Caesar (to his Imperial Advisor).
    Late in the afternoon

Will an objection be allowed? *At plus diligi.* So he said . . . on the
night the Empire burned

I've thought of the swarms of soldiers wriggling in the Empire's
tepidarium. For a while. . . .

The soul's (fragile) armor? The young man's (smooth and cool)
body in the buff

The young man taken to be one in the Celestial Sphere (soon
enough) turns to dust. By chance

The bathers half in dreams. . . . when the mountain spurting fire is,
painted (in the mural)!

Impetuously time passes. . . . Ceaselessly hot water overflowing the
bathtub (with no one in it)

The night the sweat from heavenly being's armpits smells in the
bathhouse, with someone, staring. . . .

Thou shan't talk of life's hecticness! Above your head, even the
immovable mountain sways

Should I yearn? For the day, to, arrive when above the fiery moun-
tain asleep the smoke trails

The menfolk are beaten in the bath waterfalls. Mankind is being
washed in history's torrents

Ceaselessly quaking great earth. Until that day, that mountain
becomes a fire-spurting mountain

ROMANCE OF MOON AND RIOT POLICE

After García Lorca

Los caballos negros son.
Las herraduras son negras.
Sobre las capas relucen
manchas de tinta y de cera.
—Federico García Lorca,
Romance de la Guardia Civil Española

In body odor a whiff of book burning——. Forming ranks and
keeping silent, those men

Policeman's blood can be an aphrodisiac and a poisonous liqueur.
On the night when the moon rises late

His irises so lucid as to be cruel. The new face of late a street vendor
of late a Cupid with bow and arrow

The tribe tabooing full-moon nights——. Younger brother is a gigolo,
big brother the nation's dog

Wind from the full moon? What strikes the beardless cheeks of the
members of the riot police at attention

Even the moonlight darkens a bit——. Contemptuous of the ones
hiding behind their silver-gray shields

Believe as they are forced to, that the throngs of citizens pressing
close under the moon are just pigs

The blood and sweat flowing on policemen's foreheads lodge——.
The moonlight growing clearer

The monologue that calls forth a rebellion. ——The poet the Power snuffed out was my true mate!

The authorities' heart being "nonexistent" flies toward the red-shining moon, a Molotov cocktail

INCIDENTS

Deep at night a big incident! My heart taken by a small-framed, skinny, little shit

Yet another incident? The boy I've picked up has a dimple (and a scar) on his cheek

Blissfully let me watch. The way this homeless urchin carries his body somewhat like a yakuza!

So I may die with a quiet heart? I pay for the boy with a body odor of something singed

The age of befuddlement deepens——. The perpetrator walks back to the actual spot (of the incident)

His heart deeply wounded by love? Even the arrogant–furious gigolo endlessly weeps

When will this end? This age out of line painted separately with green like camouflage?

The truth ends up unknown——. The incident the impudent orphan is said to have been involved in

The cruel fact. That as a human I shouldn't be dead but live on in the degenerate world

This must also be an incident I mutter to myself. Morning, having awaken from torment

YOUNGER BROTHER'S FATHER

TRANSLATOR'S NOTE:

In *The Tale of Genji*, Genji the Shining Prince loves many women, among them Fujitsubo, his father Emperor Kiritsubo's second wife. Kiritsubo chose Fujitsubo as his consort because she resembled the woman he truly loved, Genji's mother, who died not long after giving birth to him. The result of the illicit sexual liaison is Reizei, even though officially he is born as the emperor's tenth son.

In 1999 the Japanese Ministry of Finance announced that the design for the back of a special ¥2,000 bill to mark the year 2000 would use a picture depicting a scene in Book 37 ("Suzumushi") of the *Tale of Genji Pictorial Scroll* where one moonlit night Genji visits Onna San-no-miya, his half-niece and his second wife, then, as invited, goes to see Reizei, now a retired emperor, in his mansion where they have a moonlight banquet till dawn, composing poetry. The ministry's decision created a disbelieving fascination among some aficionados. As Ishii put it, "Does this mean that a secret 1000 years ago is now officially sanctioned?" The result was his sequence "Younger Brother's Father" (*Otōto no chichi*).

It may be noted that *suzumushi* (*Meloimorpha japonica*), "bell insect," in those days in fact referred to what today is called *matsumushi* (*Xenogryllus marmoratus*), "pine insect." Both "bell insects" and "pine insects" appear in this sequence as they are named.

> 'Tis thee, my self, that for myself I praise,
> Painting my age with beauty of thy days.
> —William Shakespeare, *Sonnet 62*

Blindly bell insects trill. The man who loved his younger brother (as if he were his father)

Well, you know! Because his soul has a wound (hard to heal) he comports himself elegantly

The day there was the report, "She gave birth to a boy," his life
    became autumnal——

A son in love with his mother makes her bear a child because of
    mother, ... at least in his heart, they say

Father's son is my son · my son is someone else's, so, compassionate
    former emperor is sin's son

"What's called sin becomes more beautiful as time passes," they say,
    that fallacy,   beautiful

Love made once in the past, right! And a new bank note with
    which to atone for it for tomorrow

Cracked memory of trysts. Stepmother resembling actual mother,
    in fact, (may be actual mother)

Which fate you are to escape from single-mindedly deepening sky
    fascinating in an imperial visit

Faithless calling younger brother, son. As night deepens like (step)
    mother autumn I miss

Gay and intriguing. Calling pine insect (pining for mother) bell
    insect (even more) faithlessness

A man who's reliant on himself, so, he despises himself. . . . the
    moon, rises some what

Peering into the mirror? No sir younger brother and older brother
    tonight, no different

Penalty for what I thought horrible, is, it, he suddenly thinks. Now
(!) insects' trills stop

Because of the sins (of each one) that overlay the story's (more)
beautiful, as, I, close, it

THE MAN'S TONGUE

To the memory of Jean Genet

Nous n'avions pas fini de nous parler d'amour.
Nous n'avions pas fini de fumer nos gitanes.
On peut se demander pourquoi les Cours condamnent
Un assassin si beau qu'il fait pâlir le jour.
    —Jean Genet, *Le Condamné à mort*

The scar in my palm, incurable   at the orphanage upon a hill at
the edge of town they turn on the light

An illegitimate child with the mark of the beast was abandoned is
all   All's right with the world

Choking with streetwalkers' sweats and souring raw garbage the
moon this evening   on and off

A regret even more like a crime——   a blond scallywag, kneels, the
evening darkness

Somersault the boy's so to be called   the lily that's also the rose
the key that's also the keyhole

Young men two?   three?   In perspiring nakedness the summer
night has turned light

Sea with golden light cast over it I would keep a brawny sailor
together with his parrot

The male prostitute's callowness—— the fire of the cigarette held
in his scarlet lips gleams and darkens

Blood in his mouth   fearing the lust in his palm a passing devil
bends forward uncertain

The man condemned to death talks of murders in prison, his
exploits   ——It is a star-studded night

A scream then a silence afterward skims over from roof to room,
moon, moonlight surreptitious

Heart already rotten   nevertheless,   the fiery lust for an unborn
beautiful boy intently hidden

A male passing by casts his fragrant night sweats   the secular
beauty betrayed

I'd like to lick with a cat's tongue—— the honey-colored wet skin
of the stevedore at the dock

Fog over the sea   in my notebook black stains of regret   quietly
the night lightens

The glory is and yes roseate—— for the kneeling poet the tattooed
goddess of poetry

The dazzle of the sun!   A saint in a mystery play, has eyes like
those of the beast

I have an ambition to perish at the edge of a star-studded field——
at a midday that is too bitter

Oed' und leer das Meer.   The beautiful rascal what mark does he
have

The younger brother runs away, body light, and left alone is his
maternal half-brother

The young man's sweat, hot——   At the center of the heavenly fire
(solemnly) the sun wavers

Thinking of catching rare insects I've come out to the field where
half-naked soldiers are all muddy

A boy talks about a revolution——   his dainty waist and fists and
saliva in his mouth

The spiral of the fire of a cigarette passed around under the moon,
the field for battle quiets down

Death is the pleasure just once   ——thus the daybreak color of
the tongue of the man I love

TOKYO = SODOM
OR SNIFFING A YOUNG MAN

> Kaori is so fragrant as not like a scent of this world, so mysterious
> that when he shifts a little, the whiff from him carries so far in the
> wind you feel as if you can smell his scent a hundred steps away.
>
> —Murasaki Shikibu, *The Tale of Genji*

Sodom in heaven   nay   Sodom on earth—— you look up and the
    city's all colonnades of light

Martyr's pomegranatelike wounds   you say, and the bar also turns
    into a   catacomb

Looking for father   or for whom? Reflected (upside down) in a glass
    a constellation

Sour saliva seeps up. . . .   resembling sin (in the pot some beast's)
    intestines are boiling

The young ones (though men) paint eyebrows dazzlingly green as
    the night has deepened

In the night street of sirens. . . . I call out and stop a youth (in plain
    dress) wet behind the ears

Ask the false moon no less—— how much is the value of the boy
    with a pigeon chest

Abloom and fragrant (overhanging) chrysanthemum. Under its
    shadow I pick up, a (brand-new) Croix de Guerre

Mad am, I mad am . . . . in the rain I turn a man (who happens to
    pass by) inside out

The make of the sword that the naked warrior has on him is, silver.
    What he wears is (bitter) body odor

The one I'm grappling with——   is God? Touching the bone on
    the young man's thighs, my hot hand

In the mist of the scent of hay.   ——For what reason my name? So
    asks in response, the man

(Though a counterfeit virtue) the virtue pours in. . . . Eromenos,
    rolls into undisclosed love

The soul is (fertilely) fragrant. Fragrantly (from his skin) seeps out.
    Little by little.

Rolls, over. . . . The young man, wafts fragrance. . . . Like the fragrance
    of the clay beaten in the rain

The way he sleeps with face down negligently——   The youth (even
    to the eye) fragrant

From the shower, the morning spurts out. . . . before that. . . . every
    corner of your body, I sniff

III

SUMMER NIGHT—TWO DUETS

i. *Boy Waiter and Poet Customer*

> Und da wird es Mitternacht seyn,
> Wo du oft zu früh ermunterst,
> Und dann wird es eine Pracht seyn
> Wenn das All mit mir bewunderst.
> —Johann Wolfgang von Goethe,
> *Sommernacht*

Give me a liquor fiery as fire   this summer night I'm silly drunk
     would like to get drunker

Brought the drink gently touched the customer's hand and went
     away   that summer waiter

A transferred scent of flowering chestnut scent   what on earth did
     the boy tell of whom

Smoke stings my eyes   the boy damsel first asks for a ciggy in my
     red pack the import

What will it be like to be drunken like gods   won't we be united
     like gods this night

I place my own ear on my boy's naked belly and I listen   so clearly
     rustles his life

It's as if the liquor scorched my throat and still I state this   ——Every-
     thing is lovely

A beautiful dream?   The summer night lightens and this morning
     already a cicada-shower of light

ii. *The Song of Brew Man and Sailor*

> Imprisoned by the sorrow you create
> you weep, do you, young man.
> —Kitahara Hakushū, *Mold of Sake*

Intermittent and yet sharp a singing voice. Who is it crossing the
canals in twilight?

Not an utter quietude yet leisurely darkening a row of houses the
sake-brewhouses

From the gleam of the poling man's upper arm, I know   this a
night of stars and the moon

Soon as he casts off the mooring line his wake follows the young
sailor giving birth to a starry night

The boatman stands on land yet his skin faintly smells of a fragrance
of the sea

Choking with sake fragrance filling the sake storehouse the sake-
brewer has a love child, does he?

The man about to light his untipped cigarette   his face set with
such a sinful menace

Pigeon-breasted seaman's apron   mother sewed it, older sister has
washed it till its indigo fades

He with a young lonesome heart has yet to be in love with no one
except his flesh and blood

His backbone and her brows straight   the older sister still stubbornly
    refuses to be a bride

What dream should a boatman have   for three days he hasn't
    returned to his house on a steep bank

Don't ask who's brewed this sake   the bachelor the brewer has a
    certain criminal record

In the darkness suddenly a man rises   violence hidden yet he still
    emanates a fragrance

Tonight what flower to bloom?   As if the stars at the rim of the
    water on a water planet fall

Drunken with stars as if drunken with a scent of something tonight
    slightly sways one side of town

How difficult to fathom our life! This summer night a certain man
    walks closer, to, a man

Coming out of the darkness and falling into the water a streak of
    firefly has mated a wind

As something with which to illuminate a new sin deep at night the
    moon silently   begins to rise

Under the moon turning blue the sailor sleeps as if dead   on the
    moon too there's a sea it is said

The pang in a heart with no one beside   there is a cigarette thrown
    in the water at daybreak

Begin to extend a pole of regret to him   Young the sailor awakes
now this morning by himself

The day breaks and it's still quiet for a while in this part of town
fragrant the moon white gleams

A NIGHT SONG SUNG AS IF MUMBLING AIMLESSLY IN THE ELEPHANT

> In the South Suburbes at the Elephant
> Is beſt to lodge: I will beſpeake our dyet,
> Whiles you beguile the time, and feed your knowledge
> With viewing of the Towne, there ſhall you haue me.
> —William Shakespeare,
> *Twelfe Night, or What You Will*

A man waits for a man oh pity as the day ends in the Elephant in
the outskirts of town

With a poet singing of himself on his own as if wisely the moon has
also appeared

Though this is far from Kyiv where the bells ring let us talk about
the edges of my heart

Count them and count them and still the winter stars multiply
your clothes-swollen shoulders the width

Giving birth itself is unhappiness; nevertheless the one who was
my love now has a child

Could our lives also dye rosy? A white-clad butcher slices the meat apart

To call you a boy your height   although your soul is still green

The dead is also a boy   the boy choir of a Requiem,   sings in chorus

Snake strawberries also summer thistles   what do birds eat coming
to my garden at daybreak and sing

Cooled the horse is there   come evening various hungers torment me

Summer festival,   will it end tomorrow   youths with belly-covers
are silly ones and wise men

Amateur sumo wrestlers' youth   their souls, to call them that
they're excessively naked

The citrus the boxer rubs into his chest its fragrance too bitter in
this evening dark

My lust at long last having grown faint then autumn wind the day
after Kenji Anniversary

I strike a match strike it but it doesn't catch fire: once in the past in
the offing here there was a naval battle

It's as if the River of Heaven were sinking noisily —when I call out,
O thou sea!

Chasing the Galaxy I throw myself into it   —shouting, *repetenda*
que numquam terra, vale!

A purple chrysanthemum easily decays though I don't call myself a
postwar child

Musicians have no wives or children they say; faintly night by night
comes a scent of ginger lilies

Snow-white bush clover has scattered away   the word love being
a word that pierces my heart

Momentary love at once is to be momentary ash   my,   love,   is
finished

The backyard has cosmos all over it   the newly appointed teacher
     is a bachelor and with a child

For my child with a cold I make kudzu soup he says but the father
     is no old-school poet

There was a horned owl with one blind eye   on the day sleet was
     falling in the zoo

Heart already withered with frost though I visit a monochromatic
     ield of graves all alone

The closed mountain must be snowy   toward the evening I alone
     rub a blue inkstick newly arrived

Someone should be killing someone this snowy night I single-
     mindedly rub an inkstick

The fresh tea the first sip, the second sip, and things all begin to
     move with the third sip

Is there a city on the floor of the sea?   Someone utterly unknown
     calls me to stop at dusk

The nō finale having ended trouble-free this evening I have scooped,
     colorless water in a crystal bowl

With a bunch of black grapes in front of me I think   of some-
     thing like, quiet death

Deep in the night I still hear a faint singing voice   has the one I've
     been waiting for arrived?

DANTE PARK, MANHATTAN
Past seven on a winter night, from the 66th Street subway stop to
the METROPOLITAN OPERA HOUSE

> fertur cita gurgite classis,
> et tandem laeti notae advertuntur harenae
> — Publius Vergilius Maro, *Aeneis,* Liber V

The crime of stabbing you stabbing me: stepping off the subway
I've become a man who forms his shadow

Why doubt myself still? Though the cape jasmine on my collar
(yes!) is an artificial flower

Out in the city the most dedicated apostles go crazy they say —
This is the very wilderness

The shadow of two together not moving blooms. Enveloped
(besides) with white exhalations

The bronze poet fearfully fearfully (Ah!) I look up at as if he were
like a dead man with a crime

An angel without wings? Or a white-haired girl? The one, who
trotted through the plaza

Brushing past me, head hung, a flock of souls pass (dressed up for
the occasion, pass)

To the opera, to the ballet, pronto! Time is being lost (in this City,
in particular)

I'm, am, looking up at the water soaring over water. Regarding
myself as an unbridled knight

Flocks of mink-fur-clad old ladies jostle, I.... Very elegantly jostle,
I saw

Artificial lights give me shadows. Numerous pale shadows that
scatter as dust!

Climb up the crimson flight of stairs as if clinging to it, so say, those
pale shadows

A golden-haired girl and a cerulean-haired youth, they, I see, are
mother and son,

besides between their eyebrows (paired!) new scars. Scars healed
by the chandelier fire?

Or else ash? Or else a stigma? Joyfully I forgive your sin, so declares
his forehead

The Creation is close. The lights that quietly climb up, and, the
blessings that pour down

If there were a spot of green in the human heart, if there were, if
there, ah!

For the people who are sunken in the abyss of remorse, the first
sound of music rings out

Raising the forbidden golden curtain, the deities (the sinful dead
people) smile

Singing dead one, dead one, dead one! Will the day come when I,
the one alive, am to be saved?

CONCERNING A MODEST APPETITE

Triptych

Betting My Honey-Containing Life

The Day of Error, should I call, it? Five kinds of tart I ate at the very end of lunch

A piece of cake that heals even the scar on my soul? Strawberries, and, cream, added, to it?

I ain't no young man so what thoughtlessness! "I love wine ♥ I love cookies too ♥" I say?

The sugar (in fact!) is a horrifying white powder. Look, here, again, another, addict. . . .

Does a sweet tooth have any rationality? Even if the evening sky glows buttery and honey colors?

The serious attention given to the dessert menu⟶ Like, a, fearless, warrior

I'd even, sell my soul! If it were for a chocolate soufflé baked in infernal flames!

I eat up all the sweets after the dessert. Bringing up dead people for gossip, I the one alive. . . .

I dedicate to the Goddess of Sugar! Both this dulled spirit, and, this fattened flesh

Today again, I eat, sweets. . . . Betting my life containing an abundance
of honey!

In Thicket

The (swaying) door called *noren.* . . . I swish it aside dashingly 'cause
I'm no man of rank, see!

Sobamiso and *dashi-maki-tamago, wasabi-imo.* . . . All appetizers
for the joys in the afterlife

A steamer of green bamboo. Though I'm a man with no chance in
the game of this life. . . .

Together with faintly bitter memories I've slurped up *sobakiri.*
Making a sharp sound

Days of longing like a hidden marsh go by. . . . I don't deny it, no
way. This scent of the "single stroke" either

'Cause this evening the world looks like a farce, shall I, laugh? As I
slurp up the soba soup

That's the second floor of a soba restaurant where they gathered,
see! Ōishi and forty-odd other men

Every time, yeah, In the Thicket! Be it a historical event, or the lives
of the downtrodden

There is, the melancholy to sweep aside, but (for now) I order (in
addition) duck-*namban*

A (single) letter I entrusted the blind messenger with ——Tomorrow
again in Thicket, or, in Sandbox!

Eating All the Tasmanian Oysters

The sea washed up by the storm since last night is bluer. Than the
dark dyeing with Indian indigo

In the atmosphere clear and (a bit) salty. . . . I first, eat, just one. An
oyster of smallish size

We've come to a faraway green island (beyond the equator). To
devour oysters. . . .

With a close friend, with his wife, the three of us surround a table.
So, small, we, love, it, don't we?

Thou shall not seek the bliss of life in food. Thou shall not (yes,
never!) say such a thing

A man single-mindedly devouring oysters is like a (wild) conqueror
of the ocean sea, isn't he!

Beyond this sea is a continent covered with ice. Darkness too soars
up, they, say. . . . .

You pick it up, and the light, brims. . . . The flesh of oyster has such
(how shall I put it!) sensuous gray

Forever the ecstasy remains fresh. Here, again, he brings us, another,
plate of silver

Suppose we devour all the raw oysters on this island. . . . I'll be led.
To where the stars sleep

SELF-PORTRAITS WITH
THE SEVEN DEADLY SINS

> pereat dies in qua natus sum et nox in qua
> dictum est conceptus est homo
>
> —Liber Iob 3:3

Self-Portrait with the Sin of Pride

Who, is that singing loudly? As if he has taken on (all the) sufferings
of mankind?

That's me! If not with Okai Takashi. . . . but shall I compete at least
with Statius?

I mouth the names of predecessors. Solemnly (as if I were their
beloved disciple)

The one-thousand-year history of tanka isn't a burden on me, and
the books I love are Loeb's. . . .

I write only for myself. Even if the work becomes (in the end) a
false graveyard, you know!

Self-Portrait with the Sin of Avarice

My heart, reels, reels. . . . 'Cause there are too many books I have
(yet) to read (in the world)

Like a prisoner I yearn. For the (landscapes I haven't seen) of the
countries I've never been to

On a winter night, that tale. . . . Weeping I will listen, to an adventure
  that isn't mine

Raging wildly my heart. Both time and space (my share of them)
  being so little so little. . . .

I'll wish for a transmigration (that I can't enjoy my life, of which
  there is only one!)

Self-portrait with the Sin of Lust

I've lived single-mindedly, that, I wouldn't, say. . . . I'm just, short
  of, secrets, is, all

True love you say? I didn't know, maybe! Though I've been in
  unconventional love. . . .

In my heart, someone's lover, someone's spouse. . . . Just thinking
  about them is a sin I know

To mate with the great sky, to sleep with the great sea. . . . No, with
  mankind, is, the best I can manage

It vanishes at once, a double rainbow. (Even) more fleeting than my
  (day-to-day) lust

Self-portrait with the Sin of Wrath

The reason for my boundless wrath? 'Cause stupid, see, human
  beings are inexhaustible in this world

Of a slaughter, That's splendid, the man whistles. . . . at the jersey figure I'm furious

My heart will grow coarse. When I think, of the hearts of those fellows grown coarse

Avert my eyes, I can't, do that! From the gods' arrogance, or from society's shamelessness. . . .

Won't, even be, a consolation! Even if mankind destroyed itself (because of its stupid acts)

Self-portrait with the Sin of Gluttony

Appetite stirs at daybreak. For the moment I eat (three) figs that are (ripe)

My heart can't remain calm. When the blood-colored, wines, are, vinted, every year. . . .

My favorite *pigeonneau fermier rôti*. Their blood compared with the blood of fallen soldiers, is cute!

This world (like me) is a big glutton, it is! Digesting (humans) innocently as it goes. . . .

The history of mankind is in short a history of cannibalism. On the great earth, ah, young blood!

Self-portrait with the Sin of Envy

Fire-colored, wings, of angels! They are what the humans (of course, I) are devoid of. . . .

These don't either! The thick, arms, of the fireman who's climbing the emergency stair case to heaven

Not even these! Announcing myself as a poet. . . . the words, I alone, have made alive. . . .

Mankind can destroy itself sure! If (I)'m not fortune's favorite son. . . .

The aquamarine, wings, of Satan! Those lost in advance, even, I'm envious of

Self-portrait with the Sin of Sloth

Ceaseless rain. . . . I don't know what to do with this heart that hasn't opened up even once

The love letter I wrote in purple ink. . . . In the end I didn't mail it. Because of the rain

Though a battle turmoil isn't far my heart tonight is wet with rain, through and through. . .

I dislike human beings. I press my lips that are turning cold against the (rainy) windowpane

Rain, may you not stop! To die, or to live, either is too much bother today, don't you see

A HUNDRED FLOWERS FELL.
SO I HEARD, SO I SAW. . . .

A sacred story? Surely it is! The one that (the girl, tonight) narrates
to her brother. . . .

That she was rescued (by a young knight resembling her brother,
from a fire-breathing sea dragon)

That she poured a frothing wine (believing it was an aphrodisiac)
into his crystal wineglass

A drop of blood on her fingertip! Shall I call her a dove? because of
the purity of the blood?

The braver he is the worse the fate that awaits him, is that the truth?
In her brother's future?

Big brother whose face foretells young death. Though he bragged,
"I just was having a dream". . . .

Words we shouldn't believe. . . . Who said, "See you, again"? Said,
"I'm sure to see you"

The ritual before sleep does resemble that before death. . . . And
after that, what?

A conventional metaphor this but the fingers are like white fish.
What do they play with?

—*I pray you, brethren, do not so wickedly*, you said. . . . You are the
worst! so said the girl

—*I have two daughters which have not known man*, are the terrible (Biblical) words

Crisis for the tribe! For the sacrifice a hundred virgins and (in the world to come) their bridegrooms. . . .

The palace room dark as the womb. . . . The princess likes her brother (better than anyone else)

In the margin of her (big brother's) diary the sister reads full of curiosity, there's a stain. . . .

That there was a boy among the tributes from a distant land, that, a legend from long ago

The big brother who has his sister clinging to him, the rogue, his rosy, upper arm

In time the flower scatters. The girl wants to bear (her brother) a child, a wish understandable

To become a mother while a virgin, to dream such a thing is what's good about his sister

She who has never been ill finally falls ill (the worst (the sweetest) disease) called love

That thing (his sister) wrapped in a newspaper and abandoned (quite heavy), that is, what?

—*Laisse-moi, mon bien-aimé! laisse-moi partir!* The one singing that, who's she?

A word of reconciliation with the world? —*Laisse-moi devenir une étoile!* or so it goes. . . .

The shadow prostrating before the altar is a girl (who, in truth!) may no longer be that. . . .

Must be no more than a phantom. —*O Marie, Reine du Ciel!* Her compassion, too

For that, the crown. . . . For what is likely to be just one wedding (and one funeral) in life

A snow-white selfless heart, and, a rose-colored heart in love. What side are we to take?

Girls' vernal hearts! *Thou shalt not allow them to bloom with flowers, to vie*, it is said

Love is always transient. *Love that lasts for a moment turns to ashes in a moment*, you know!

To be lost in the light of the sun. Both the rising tower, and the love that burns us. . . .

Struck by lightning (at night) the tower soars. Yes, until the day it collapses, as you know!

And the Lord came down to see the city and the tower. That alone (!) drove Him into baseless fury. . . .

The sunrise is still faraway. Yet the youth is close to the Lord, shall I say that? Or not?

Can't wait, for the morning. Though we may be able to abandon (something) before then

The word that links this world to the world to come, is what? I ask, in a cool tree shade

"See you!" he says. . . . Probably the world to come has neither a waterfall, nor a shining sea

Music ended, the east wind weakened . . . a hundred flowers fell. So I heard, and so I saw. . . .

Over there, a waterfall. . . . Abandoned in the plain what should the girl hold up, what?

That after the spring day turns to darkness life should continue (even then! for a long time!). . . .

You know what his sister said? —The past? I left it in my room, I forgot to bring it here!

Can't be free, you know! The twin big brother and kid sister (and their double) fate

Diseased sea that goes on suppurating. . . . No one has anything like a method of healing it

On earth a babel of words. . . . There's no longer that tower or that tower. Or that tower!

Why was the Lord furious? ——Yes, that's because He had never seen a dream. He never had.

On the earth after the Flood they are like ants, or so it is said. The
Lord's lovely children

Once it existed, but no more. The Tower of Babel of arrogant people
... or the Twin Towers....

...*et idcirco vocatum est nomen* ... (or so you read in the Bible) ...
eius Babel.... (!)

Since it escaped collapse the city (although it was abandoned) has
been called Babel

The sister prays for her brother. In the graveyard that isn't far from
the sea or from the plain

At the vine-crawling ancestral grave —Something bitter as everyone
knows? Don't ask that

Listening, meditate to death. The nonexistent sister narrating to
her nonexistent brother

BATHHOUSE

Abraham autem consurgens mane ubi steterat prius cum Domino
intuitus est Sodomam et Gomorram
et universam terram regionis illius
viditque ascendentem favillam de terra quasi fornacis fumum
—Liber Genesis, 19: 27–28

Poi si rivolse e parve di coloro
che corrono a Verona il drappo verde
per la campagna; e parve di costoro
quelli che vince, non colui che perde.
—Dante Alighieri, *Inferno*,
Canto XV: 121–124

Since I wandered out into twilight town my body   has been filled
with sleepiness   and fragrant

Already my body is tired out with desire   probably so is my soul

Out on the town dazzling with false lights I knew   the atmo-
sphere is too heavy

Dreams sunken in wine cups: this body too had days when it was
humans' innocent son

Satiated yet starved, starved and yet. . . . .   tonight what kind of
pleasure   shall I buy

Probably this is insanity   nay   growing clearer and clearer is my
sanity tonight

Wearied out of even smiling powerlessly tonight again I go to visit
a house of ill repute

(The custom of likening stars to eyes) over the town of pleasure I
  imagine a starry sky

My indecisions being deep..... from street to street I go the smells
  of things even darker

"Only the shops selling humans prosper in (this town" I wait for
  the day to wrap it in flames)

Ra-ri-re-ru children crouching by the roadside! Humans are creatures
  attacked by death

My heart painfully pains when I think of mankind as a species
  going extinct

Getting together yet remaining silent these beautiful devils • those
  despicable angels and their ilk

Coming out on the town of death to meet we each of us are led by
  each's own solitude

Bronze automatic door   each soul in silence goes in there (as if
  wishing for death)

We all members of a family of lamentation: someone passing by
  with a whiff of gunpowder

I've given a modicum of money in exchange for a key (this key is
  like ice in my palm)

Bearded man with bearded man   the next morning Peter is said to
  have *wept bitterly*

The scents of sweet and sour male sweats fills the locker room
    dazzlingly bright

"A locked darkness has a past" the locker door pale and creaking opens

Geese flying through an illusory sky: as if with a sigh all have taken
    their clothes off and discarded them

Only when a man becomes all naked do you know the shades of his
    life as an existential being

Mediterranean nudes!   Nay, I don't mean to boast, no, but we are
    such an elegant tribe

He draws them a little closer and lifts them   a young man's eye-
    brows (ocean!) so beautiful

By falling silent a suggestion of *déjà vu*   a dark green shadow
    crosses the man's eyelids

Within each and every one of the men desire brims up quietly (like
    the sea)

Entrapped we are   all in the prisons of lust, each one separately,
    eternally. . . .

(As if there were light at the very end of the turbulent sea) our flesh
    grows hot

If you are to die because of love you should, all the more so if it's a
    casual one-night stand

Turning to look, again, turning to look, we pass by in the colon-
    nade, our souls, our, solitudes!

Aren't our lives full of torments? The one with head down and in
thought the one asleep in a chair

We are the hollow men.... men kissing each other must be weeping
bitterly in their hearts

You face it with doglike eyes and the shower douses you with a
shout like a dog

Beaten by the rain a dog and another! Being a human and the one
inferior to a dog is beautiful

In a (lacquer-black) rubber raincoat (and becoming wet) the one
who sang in cold rain

The used tires are heavy for no reason (the young man's smiling
cheeks soiled with oil)

So you may wash away the young man's sweat and befoulment,
rain, fall   salty rain!

To pick up the soap I bend down when—   the shower pains my
skin piercingly

O hole in the wall here!   the desire to peer in is no more than a
hole you feel

(Love resembles yes the wrestling sport) the way they love each
other the men's nobility

"Mindlessness" is what kind of mind: gamboling sons are in other
words the sons of God

On the ground skylarks in heaven are grappling sons mysterious
   upside down their images

The seer's heart must be a bottomless pit (in Lancashire four thou-
   sand holes)

(The throat is yet another sexual organ) at a faint sound of gargling
   I prick up my ears

In the marble bathtub black waves rise "Long ago, in Rome there
   was a blood bath

"A policeman a soldier a firecracker-craftsman and all sunken in
   this deep hot bathtub

"Having cooked a soup of two brawny slaves . . . ." a blood-smelling
   peacock-feather fan

Red-hot iron I first thought it was: in the hot bath a man   his back
   straightened squats immersed

The Kingdom in the steam: now, the man rises from the hot
   water as a knight on pilgrimage

Ruminating on desire, the pilgrim steps away into a dense fog
   him, it is, that I run after

Hidden village of hot sand! A caravan has brought with them they
   say a slave with beautiful features

Because he was born the day of solar eclipse the black man's black
   skin is as hot as fire

Child with his hair flowing mauve: on that hair of his blows the
   hot wind savagely

Desire grows ever more heavy: even the breath I exhale may congeal
   and turn into a hot stone

The hot wind darkly resounds: face down and keeping silent these
   men   for whom do they wait

Nigra sum sed formosa. . . . so sing we the despicable   covered with
   sweat

Would I had a white birch branch   to whip my own flesh scorched
   with desire

Hapless friends filling this world: once in the field   *I ha' seen him
   eat o' the honey-comb*

Sin' they nailed him to the tree. Every friend of mine I long for as my
   heart wishes

The mind to be judged   the man's broad back seems to perspire as
   if weeping

In the city on fire the anger of fire   I secretly yearn for the day a
   rain of fire will fall

Fake cigarette we pass around to smoke: at times human beings
   yearn for death lovingly

Both my intellect and my bodily strength have somewhat numbed
   (clearly my future a blur)

(Let there be light   so I shout in my heart but) my pupils show a
   symptom of dilation

Like an ill omen it has smelled: in the darkness and half asleep a
   male body

Accursed sleep   what the man crowns on his shoulders is an
   unknown man's <head>

Riding the subway to my ear there's the word: "Thou shalt love thy
   neighbor as thyself"

In the packed car fellows are connected in secret   eye with eye,
   hand with   phallus

What is the mind to see?   In the small movie house only the seats
   at back are crowded

Desire heightens turbulent until its transmission reaches Nod (east-
   ward in Eden)

With no end in sight is God's anger: from Genesis to Revelation God
   is angry

His anger forgiven: Is that a dream   as if biting a finger I surrepti-
   tiously bite a man

Since the rain long ago stopped the creature's heart the solitude has
   dyed each and every one

Touching his heated body I find myself aggrieved (the bronco is yes
   such a noble beast)

Riding bareback and galloping through a flowering early summer forest—who's that bare warrior?

Mating we are yes beasts (both a man with golden hair and a black man)

That men also have nipples makes you sad doesn't it: bite one and blood oozes faintly

Family tree in which people die young without cease: nail clipped too deep the ring finger suddenly aches

As a human what kind of death shall I die? "A blue snake has a green life"

Gloria Patri et Filio . . . Transmitted through semen and blood, and both life and death!

My body losing weight with no reason: lately among the dead my friends increasing

Ill because of bodily desire yes   this being's no more than a pleasure vessel

My sick friend has muttered "Quick, death, come . . ." (*And I Don't Say*) my sick friend!

Would there were the means of tearing my flesh and cutting up my heart—   Life is probably darker than death

The word justice is bitter: going to die a human pants as if he were a beast

Let at least a phantom snow fall in the fiery throat   Ah!   even one
 alive one is parched

"Scatter, my, ashes, in the sea" my friend said and died, I burned
 him   on a cape full of blooming flowers

Excreting sweat still more sour than tears: are my sins ripening?

Since I saw in a phantom a mountain of cherry blossoms in full
 bloom I've despised   God

How has my heart coarsened   though my dear sea is calm with
 purple *moules*

How many times I've shed tears • repeated words *ego sum A et ω*

Its touch resembling deer skin leather. . . .   boundary between a
 new death and a new life

With fingers in a rubber glove I've touched.   The man's body as
 hot as sin

The human is a single duct (violated by angel's arm burning like
 fire)

As I devour it noisily pomegranate is sweet   a man's tongue, is far,
 sweeter

The pair of angels were (in truth!) gangbanged by the men of the
 city.   So the legend

Smoke rises from the city   why is it that my body mired in foul
 habits doesn't at once turn into salt

A man pelted by a rain of fire and running (ah) my heart resembles
    him most

Three men entangled with one another ...   *Or aspetta!* The souls
    drenched in sweat also three

Many a nude body aglow because of sin   what twines them into
    a   human rope

Hold a young man's innocent nude body tight. . . .   else tightly tie
    it up with a rope

Excelled in literary and martial arts and being a rascal besides: such
    is truly a man   among men

Blindfolded the man mutters: "When is it, that I will see, beautiful,
    stars. . . ."

Out of the bottom of the world where it falls asleep, men have
    responded, *Bald, oder nie!*

Lying at the base of the air dark and dense the men asleep   their
    breathing as they sleep!

On the seabed numberless souls of melancholy gather and sing
    Lacrimosa dies illa they say . . .

The men entangling one another and dreaming are good (in their
    armpits they store sweet sweat)

A hallucinator would call <<scorpion>>   the man who rapes a
    sleeping man as he sleeps

What kind of bird is a cuckoo? On the silent TV a video of dissection
of a human being

Falling into sleep further   According to Brueghel   *when Icarus fell
/ it was spring*

Vae unum abiit and yet at the bottom of my dark sleep there's a
shadow passing by

> et abiit primus et effudit fialam suam in terram
> et factum est vulnus saevum ac pessimum in
>   homines qui habent caracterem bestiae
> et eos qui adoraverunt imaginem eius
>
> —Apocalypsis Iohannis 16:2

I shall be too late! I chase a shadow that runs away through the
midst of my soul

New melancholy!   Needless to say though what's on my forehead
is the mark of the beast

We the ones who've come out into this world without luck (our
fingertips always fragrant of hyacinth)

A beast is slain, a beast thrives. A beast, never sheds tears

The blood that boils down rings on the sand. . . . Aren't (sinful) we
the ones to be sacrificed?

A dog's (rosy) cadaver gleams (wet in rain). A resemblance between
God and the dog

Legend from ancient times "(Each time <a species> dies) the Lord weeps with his seven eyes"

A man possesses (as a clue for having himself saved?) a dew-drenched sinful soul

(Human beings's tireless flatteries) the blind God doesn't believe in his own blindless

Solemnly (and, glitteringly) sinking! Waterfalls, cathedrals, even the Good Earth. . . .

I've dreamed of falling endlessly down through a pit tomb   my mud-covered skull

The dream resembles • a torture • there's someone licking the sole of my foot with a fiery tongue

Panting • also weeping • I • have • a dream   . . . full of dreams those who passed away had

Being in this world is like a great dream! Yet what kind of someone else's dream is this dream?

Our soul (be it of an innocent one or of a sinful one) in the end —*bangs!* ——will it disappear?

"*Ditto*" *said Tweedle* . . . / "*Ditto, ditto*"   says, says, all alone a copier that gleams deep at night

Radiantly laugh seven times   Kid brother is no simple *copy* of big brother

Only a fool knows the future they say   from one hundred years of
  pleasure to one thousand years of solitude

A man sick in summer both his sighs • and his dreams • ripening. . . .
  (This evening again a dynasty dies)

"Avoid all intercourse in the world . . ." ——And yet even yearning
  for that this lonely heart

Resembling a wood in summer night this mystifying dark heart
  (the name of the beast inhabiting my heart)

"I'm a Fawn!" it cried out. . . .   Names are covenants (besides, of
  only humans!)

In a large pot a rabbit is cooked, cooked bubbling bubble. . . .
  et efuge in Aegyptum

(Being a human that an infant ends up as) I stab at the flesh of a
  pigeon with a silver fork

The ear is yes a deep-sea oyster. It gets chewed up by gleaming teeth
  and a scarlet tongue

Piled up on the seabed! The dreams of innocent sailors too • shat-
  tered • along with their ship

The man face down (scattering false flowers on his back) will soon
  melt away

The swirling magnetic storm   *If you see kay / Tell him . . .* "Thou,
  the beast's descendants"

A tribe with <fangs> in their rectums, has grown, in the town in blood-smelling rain. They, say. . . .

Ceaseless rain O the boy I've chosen for one night's companion has canine teeth that are sharp

Humans all turn against nature. Just as they turn against blood, turn (in the end) against their fathers

Gloria Patri, et Filio, . . . Transmitted through semen and blood, and both life and death!

Dripping the blood has turned into stone / lightning transforming itself has become a blue lizard

Still! Bub! Die Augen zu! Look, the light that dances on the wall. The light is the enemy of a sinful child

Empty • oh • the • empty • cradle • rocks. . . . We do not wish to produce children

The logic that there's no human not born as a child   Put the can of ananas upside down and then open it

My body is a garment of lead!   Without this, my heart, would have an excursion, in, Crystal Heaven

The stave called gravity, ties man to the ground. To "The Promised Land" filled with defilements

In the penal colony the snow falling piling up • has imprisoned the people (the fossilized dragons)

et profugus in terra. . . . Isn't it that man is exiled to this star for eternity

A lapis lazuli snake, cuts through space, spitting fire. . . . The snake
has wings of invisible death

On this star forests burn. The forests bound up immovably by the
orbits of flying birds

Angel of emerald fury (ah) I'm the one that's pierced by those eyes!

The cursed star being also a blessed star, in the night sky a rainbow
rises

Two entangled jade-green snakes, I untangle. Indeed, the cosmos is
packed with puzzles isn't it

"Space is that is to say numerous gazes (is it?)" they say. Behold!
Starlight underwater

Dusking water planet: the seraph has <sharp claws> and <wings
of fire>

vox sanguinis fratris. . . . My soles • step • on • the moist • cold • globe

"Underfoot there is a pit" the pit into which falls the girl <also>
singing with a clear voice

"The mouth is a deep pit" the angel with bloodied wings, falls into
this

A large hole, opens up in heaven. From that hole pours in the real
darkness of space

"The moon is already about to kiss the waves" they say but the luck-less ones are all asleep

Schorach ani wenowach. . . . (Ah!) the soul's vessel is beautiful and brittle

I must be what will • once burn as fire • and turn to ashes (by the river of tears)

The moonlight is faint. . . . (Canned) snail eggs I have a blind urge to eat

Snow-white bedsheet and tablecloth   all the countless lives and deaths that have fallen into this throat

Man too is also a beast. Beasts bite at each other. . . . *Qui vous a mis dans cette fichue position?*

C'était le sacré pigeon, Philippe. Brothers are linked in blood (and further) ill of blood

Big brother! Priest! "The worst disaster in the history of mankind has arrived" is that true?

non hunc sed Barabban   So shouts the voice. Over the silent heads.

My brush disturbed, my heart even more disturbed. . . . Yes that's true! This evening, my blood grows murkier

ὡς δὲ καὶ ὀστέα νῶιν ὁμὴ σορὸς ἀμφικαλύπτοι
χρύσεος ἀμφιφρεύς, τόν τοι πόρε πότνια μήτηρ.
—Homeros, *Ilias*, Book 23, 91–92

Не рыдай Мене, Мати, the sin I cannot escape as a child (being a child)

во гробе зрящи. These bones asleep alone at the bottom of the
   dark earth, frozen

Younger brother's bones, older brother's bones. Either bones come
   from <mother's bone-colored milk>

Beautiful infant memory. —I bit mother's nipple with my teeth
   and the blood oozes out

This flesh is mother's flesh, and this soul is . . . this soul (ah) smells
   of sulfur

The breath entangled in my throat a beast's breath, I am about to
   die (or awake)

A wind rises in the daybreak darkness "At the table at the end of my
   life figs are apt. . . ."

I'd never been slapped by mother. Still now mother just slapped me
   on the cheek, "Awake!"

ecce mater tua. . . . Ah! in our world of sorrow the children as yet
   <unable to die>

What kind of bird is the *kalaviṅka*? I yearn for "the day I die in the
   arms of my mother who's dead"

A daybreak dream is one that comes true! Mother also was lost in
   the dense darkness at daybreak

Why does a human shed tears, awaking from a dream. . . . Awaking
   I hear "the sound of a walnut cracked"

The one who goes is beau. . . . / the one who's gone to the other shore is beautiful. Beautiful and strong

With whose force has the night turned light? Far away, numerous howls of dogs in the distance

Awaking from a nightmare (is Earth still safe this morning?) I return to the city of nightmare

The mist of regrets, don't clear up. . . . Sunday at ten o'clock in the morning I bury "love"

The dead are like the living / the living like the dead. . . . गत (gah-teh)! In the daybreak sky birds call

"The way is long, and difficult the road" from the prison of life to the return to nothingness

The city of morning glow resembles a town of death noiselessly burning. . . . Burn, this star!

From heaven you hear faintly. Indistinguishable star, a voice calling a star. . . . svāhā

From heaven you hear definitely   . . . svāhā! Star, human, calling, a voice   . . . svāhā

. . . svāhā!

      . . . svāhā!

            . . . svāhā!

TREETOP FLOWERS
After Li Shangyin

> spring sun at the end of sky
> end of sky sun slants over
> oriole calls like cries tears
> moisten the tallest flowers
> —Li Shangyin, "The End of Sky"
> (tr. Jeffrey Yang)

Bush warbler's voices are faraway as I awake in a dream of a sea of regrets, calm on the calm

Streaks of tears unmistakable——. On one cheek of the fireman I held in my arms all night as we slept

With a watering can I should pour on a smiling flower. Before morning the morning light

At daybreak the flower makes waves——. Will spring pay a visit, even in Ultima Thule

Tearfully I will say to the pale moonlight. Only you who are here and are alive are the spring

What we ought to do is love. One morning, in an east wind, unstintingly a youthful flower scatters

To the prisoner in a fort in a wetland sent from an ice-free port, a secret missive——. Solus Rex's

Very best measure. To pick all the flowers there are and to let all the stars there are fall

The flower high and blooming on an upper twig also falls. Faster
than sharing the pillow we've shared

All the flowers called flowers scatter. The naked mariner spreads
the sails of his boat to the island of love

SAILING INTO THE LANDSCAPE

To Claude Lorrain

> That is no country for old men.
> —W. B. Yeats,
> *Sailing to Byzantium*

Sinking world! Or is it the evening (of birds) that goes on falling soundlessly?

In the harbor numerous ships. . . . All ships stay at anchor with memories of storms

We who are not immortals. At the end of this (tear-soaked) summer, come, let us set sail

At stern at bow (Friend who killed himself!) take up a lyre that doesn't sound even if you play, sing voicelessly

To me, the one endowed with no wings (indeed) flesh is a heavy robe, wouldn't you say?

In a country where souls sing (a country in twilight!) am I to meet my mother once again?

I would learn the song (Behold! The evening sky is unfathomably clear and quiet besides)

Led by dolphins the color of evening glow I cross the sea. Noiselessly, I cross, the seas. . . .

"Ovidius, died on the Black Sea——" the news, at long last, arrives. After darkness has completely settled

The Handsome Sailor has sunk in the maelstrom. Just like a lily
   that remained in bud

The sails all burned by the stars. . . . (To tell the truth!) heroes never
   make it back home

The nightmare that utters no voice! Nay, they say. Something called
   eternity, makes no sound

Has the body perished? None of my (with a torch raised) shadow
   on the quarterdeck

Destined to stop a beer barrel the Great King's flesh. My flesh I
   shall throw into the sea

Having set sail, one night is a hundred generations——.
                         Gilded morning awakes, at the end of the sea

I'd stay in mother's womb!
                Though setting sailing again is painful
                                    and the world is dark

NOTES

THE VOID OF THE SEA

6   *only gray hair and wrinkles . . .*: From the poem "Laughing at a Boy" by Li He (790–816 AD).

8   This last tanka at the end of this sequence refers to the final volume of Mishima's tetralogy, *The Sea of Fertility*.

HIDING BEHIND A CLOUD

10   *The hibiscus curtain is warm*: From the poem "Song of Everlasting Regret" by Bai Juyi (772–846 AD). This poem, based on Emperor Xuanzong's fateful indulgence in the great beauty Yang Guifei, provides a motif for Book One of *The Tale of Genji*, "Kiritsubo," and Book Forty, "Maboroshi."

11   *Ought to be different from the usual . . .*: The penultimate sentence in "Maboroshi."

   Smoke and dust erupt in the watch towers: From Bai Juyi's, "Song of Everlasting Regret." Subsequent lines in italic are also quoted from this poem unless otherwise noted.

12   *Count on a magician*: In Bai Juyi's "Song of Everlasting Regret," "magician" refers to a Daoist who can "open up the sky, ride on the air, rush like lightning, climb into heaven, and enter the earth." In Book Forty of *Genji*: "a magician who flies through the big sky, search the whereabouts of her soul that does not appear even in dreams."

13   *Wo kommt sie her?*: "Where does it come from?" From Hugo von Hofmannsthal's *Die Frau ohne Schatten* (*The Woman without a Shadow*).

14   *Charles Swann, mort!*: "Charles Swann, dead!" From Marcel Proust's *Le Temps retrouvé* (*Time Regained*).

   Ah! where in the world is the princess?: A nurse's cry when Ukifune disappears, in Book thirty-two of Genji, *Kagerō*.

15   *Schatten zu werfen, beide erwählt!*: "Casting shadows, as we were both chosen to do!" From Hugo von Hofmannsthal's *Die Frau ohne Schatten*.

   Il était grand temps: "It is high time." From *Le Temps retrouvé* (*Time Regained*).

THE NIGHT ALL MANKIND GREW OLD

17   *There was a man, listen, Dwelt by a churchyard:* From Shakespeare's *The Winter's Tale*, Act 2, Scene 1.

I thought of those September massacres: From William Wordsworth's *The Prelude*, Book Ten.

AT THE FOOT OF POPOCATÉPETL

20   *hegemon trees:* One name for cacti in Chinese.

THE NIGHT I SLEPT WITH MY FATHER

31   *cries out to me from the ground. . .:* Allusion to Genesis 4:10.

35   *Thou art spring!:* "Du bist der Lenz." From Richard Wagner's *Die Walküre* (*The Valkyrie*).

36   *Today yes this day shall deliver, and, destroy me:* From Sophokles, *Oedipus Tyrannus* (*Oedipus the King*).

37   *In a revolution the poet died and left his epic unfinished:* Like Marcus Annaeus Lucanus and his *De Bello Civili*.

monarchomachia: From the Greek *mónarchos* + *máxē*, "one who fights against the monarch." See *Encyclopedia Britannica*: "Any member of a group of sixteenth-century French Calvinist theorists who criticized absolute monarchy and religious persecution while defending various related doctrines of ancient constitutionalism, social contract, and resistance to unjust or tyrannical government, up to and including by means of tyrannicide. The word was coined by the Scottish absolutist William Barclay, who intended it as a term of abuse."

ORESTES IN HIS OLD AGE

39   *Epigraphs:* Sophocles: "My son, my son have pity on your mother." Proust: "Let us remember that the Ancients knew no altar more sacred, surrounded by a more profound veneration and superstition, or a guarantee of more greatness and glory for the land that possessed them and had fought for them at some cost, than the tomb of Oedipus at Colonus and the tomb of Orestes at Sparta, that same Orestes whom the Furies had pursued to the feet of Apollo himself and of Athena, saying, 'We drive the parricidal son far from the altars'" (tr. Michael Wood, *Raritan*: Fall 2005).

42   *fair-skinned aunt:* Helen of Troy.

the sea has closed over them: See the last line of Canto 26 in Dante's *Inferno*.

43   *Epigraph*: Voltaire: "Scarcely had they reached the city, lamenting the death of their benefactor, when they felt the earth tremble under their feet. The sea swelled and foamed in the harbor, and beat to pieces the vessels riding at anchor. Whirlwinds of fire and ashes covered the streets and public places; houses fell, roofs were flung upon the pavements, and the pavements were scattered. Thirty thousand inhabitants of all ages and sexes were crushed by the ruins." (Anonymous translator, 1898)

44   *Epigraph*: Schiller: "Since gunpowder was invented angels have ceased to fight" (tr. G. H. Noehden and J. Stoddart).
    No souls came from Hiroshima u know: From James Merrill's *The Book of Ephraim.*

45   *I am the enemy you killed, my friend*: From Wilfred Owen's "Strange Meeting."
    Epigraph: Chironnup Yaieyukar ("Fox Deity Sings About Itself"): "The cape of the country, above the cape of God was I seated" (from the Ainu of Chiri Yukie). "Haikunterke Haikoshitemturi" is a phrase in Ainu called a "sakahe," which refers to words in a chant or song of unknown meaning but which are retained for function and sound. In this case the phrase identifies this particular fox song.

TO THE TANKA POET

49   *Epigraph*: Prévert: "Oh Barbara / It's rained all day on Brest today / As it was raining before / But it isn't the same anymore / And everything is wrecked / It's a rain of mourning terrible and desolate" (tr. Lawrence Ferlinghetti).

51   *Brest*: Military port in the west of France.

52   *mulier ecce filius tuus*: "Woman behold your son." (John 19:26)

53   *Mais où sont les neiges d'antan?*: "But where are last year's snows?" From François Villon's "Ballade des dames du temps jadis."
    The rain's like boasting: From a poem by Li He.

54   *À quoi bon, un duo?*: "What good is a duet?" From Jean Giraudoux's *Sodome et Gomorrhe.*
    He sent (poetry) out of the overthrow: Allusion to Genesis 19:29.
    Le monde disparaît. Le rideau tombe: "The world disappears. The curtain falls." (Last stage direction in Act II in Jean Giraudoux's *Sodome et Gomorrhe*).

HONEYBEE'S WINGBEAT

55   *You were once, discarded by lute-verse-wine friends*: From Bai Juyi's poem "Three Friends of the Northern Window."

CLIPPING MY PUBIC HAIR   WASHING A HORSE

This sequence uses Okai's tanka plus his name as an acrostic running forward and Tsukamoto's tanka plus his name as an acrostic running backward. The forward acrostic is composed of the first character of the top half of each vertical line; the backward acrostic, which starts at the end of the poem, is composed of the first character of the bottom half of each vertical line. No attempt was made to reproduce this in the translation.

ABOUT THE GLOVE AND POCKETS

67   *Je tiens la reine!*: "I hold the queen!" From Stéphane Mallarmé's "L'Après-midi d'un faune."

WISTERIAS IN THE WILD, OR A VIEW OF MY SMALL STUDY

71   *Masaoka Shiki*: (1867–1902), tanka and haiku reformer who stressed the idea of *shasei*—"copying" exactly what you see—in both poetic forms. *Songs of Bamboo Villa* (*Take no sato uta*) is a collection of his tanka.
    Red Rome, and, green Hellas: In the Loeb Classical Library, the volumes of Latin literature are bound in red, those of Greek literature in green.
    The shoe that Lucy lost: "The Lost Shoe" in Walter de la Mare's *Rhymes and Verses: Collected Poems for Young People.* "Poor little Lucy / By some mischance / Lost her shoe / As she did dance — / 'Twas not on the stairs / Not in the hall," etc.
    Java, China, and lamped Japan: Ibid. "And still she patters / In silk and leather, / O'er snow, sand, shingle, / In every weather; / Spain, and Africa, / Hindustan, / Java, China, / And lamped Japan," etc.

72   *audience color: yurushi-iro*, one of the colors specified by the Imperial Court.

73   *Those blooming pliantly long and deep are, lovely*: A passage in Sei Shōnagon's *Pillow Book* (*Makura no sōshi*) praising wisteria.
    Wisteria flowers, deep in color, their clusters long: Passages in the "long song" (*nagauta*) for the dance *Wisteria Daughter* (*Fujimusume*) performed by a female impersonator (*onnagata*).

74   *rì jiàn gū fēng shuǐ shàng fú*: "I see a solitary peak afloat above the water." A line from Zhang Shuo's poem that is also its title. Here the water refers to Lake Dongting, the Yantze River's flood basin famous in Chinese painting and poetry.

      Brother Jūrō, why is it that you do not respond?: A question asked in the nō play *The Soga in Night Vendetta* (*Youchi Soga*). The Soga brothers, Jūrō and Gorō, avenge their father at night. They succeed in their aim, but in the melee that immediately follows, the older brother Jūrō is killed, and the younger brother Gorō is captured and executed. The play is based on actual events that took place in 1193 on the outskirts of Mt. Fuji.

75   *Looked after by my son in a previous life*: From the jōruri/kabuki *Iga-goe dōchū sugoroku* (*On the Road Going Over Iga Pass Together: Back-gammon*). Based on a vendetta in 1634 touched off by a man killing another man who rejected his love.

      Who will make the sounds of waves?: Usually Mt. Fuji is painted as soaring beyond a bay.

      Decet timeri Caesarem: Nero's statement: "It befits Caesar to be feared." From *Octavia*, attributed to Seneca. It's the only *praetexta* (garb) play that has survived.

76   *At plus diligi*: Seneca's response—"But more to be loved"—in *Octavia*.

ROMANCE OF MOON AND RIOT POLICE

77   *Epigraph*: Lorca: "The horses are black. / The horseshoes are black. / Stains of ink and wax / shine on their capes" (tr. A. S. Kline).

YOUNGER'S BROTHER FATHER

81   *"She gave birth to a boy"*: From "Momiji no Ga" ("The Autumn Excursion"), Book Seven of *The Tale of Genji*.

      my son is someone else's: Kaoru, one of Genji's sons, is actually the son of his wife Onna San-no-miya and Kashiwagi.

      Love made once in the past: In "Momiji no Ga," *The Tale of Genji*, facing Kiritsubo's refusal to show him his son soon after his birth, Genji composes a poem: "How is it that because of the love we once made we must be separated like this in this world?"

Gay and intriguing: In Book 38, "Suzumushi" ("Insect"), Genji visits Onna San-no-miya: "Yes, among the insects trilling, pine insects began to tinkle and it was gay and intriguing."

No sir younger brother and older brother tonight, no different: In "Suzumushi" as Reizei receives Genji in his mansion, there is a description of Reizei's face: "As he grew older and his face more composed, he looked no different [from Genji]—even more so [if that was possible]."

82 *Penalty for what I thought horrible*: In Book 35, "Kashiwagi" ("Oak Tree"), when Genji learns that Onna San-no-miya has given birth to a male child, he thinks of his secret sexual liaison with Fujitsubo and muses: "How strange, this must be a penalty for what I thought horrible."

THE MAN'S TONGUE

83 *Epigraph*: Genet: "We haven't yet finished speaking of love / we haven't yet finished smoking our cigs / we wonder why the Courts condemn / a murderer so beautiful / he pales the day" (tr. Mark Spitzer).
   mark of the beast: See Revelation 16:2 and 19:20.
   the key that's also the keyhole: The word order of this tanka is reversed in the original.

85 *Oed' und leer das Meer*: "Bleak and empty, the sea." "[V. *Tristan und Isolde*,] III, verse 24," as T. S. Eliot notes in *The Waste Land*.

TOKYO = SODOM   OR SNIFFING A YOUNG MAN

86 *Sodom in heaven*: Tsukamoto Kunio's tanka in his collection *Seisan Zu* (*Picture of Astral Dining*): "Smell of Sodom in heaven, sweat on earth, you, men, who strike a match against your Texas boots."
   Croix de Guerre: The medal that Robert de Saint-Loup accidently drops in a brothel in Proust's *À la recherche du temps perdu*.

87 *Mad am, I mad am*: A palindrome that appears on page 132 of the original text of Joyce's *Ulysses*: "Madam, I'm Adam. And Able was I ere I saw Elba."

SUMMER NIGHT—TWO DUETS

91 *Epigraph*: Goethe: "That's the midnight hour, when often / You wake early from your dreaming: / Then we'll gaze at it together, / See the whole great star-world gleaming" (tr. David Luke).

92   *Kitahara Hakushū*: (1882–1942), extolled as a national poet; grew up in Yanagawa, a seaside town known for its crisscrossing canals. Hakushū's family were sake brewers.

A NIGHT SONG SUNG AS IF MUMBLING AIMLESSLY IN THE ELEPHANT

96   *Cooled the horse*: "Cooling a horse"—or "washing a horse"—is a seasonal phrase in haiku.

repetenda que numquam terra, vale!: "Farewell, O Earth, to which I shall nevermore return!" (tr. Frank Justus Miller). From Ovid's *Metamorphoses*, XIII.

DANTE PARK, MANHATTAN

98   *Epigraph*: Virgil: "the ships rode swiftly on the swells. / At last, with joy, they landed on familiar shores" (tr. Shadi Bartsch).

CONCERNING A MODEST APPETITE

101   *Thicket*: *Yabu*, name of a superlative soba restaurant in Tokyo. Also alludes to Kurosawa Akira's film *Rashōmon,* which is based on two short stories by Akutagawa Ryūnosuke, "Rashōmon" and "In the Thicket" ("Yabu no naka").

"single stroke": *Hitomoji*, a ladies' term for the scallion.

Ōishi and forty-odd other men: Legend has it that the Forty-Seven Samurai, led by Ōishi Kuranosuke, gathered for soba in preparation for a predawn attack. It was a cold night.

duck-namban: Soba dunked in hot soup with duck.

102   *Sandbox*: *Sunaba*, another superlative soba restaurant in Tokyo.

SELF-PORTRAITS WITH THE SEVEN DEADLY SINS

103   *Epigraph*: Book of Job 3:3: "Let the day perish wherein I was born, And the night *in which* it was said, There is a man child conceived" (KJV).

A HUNDRED FLOWERS FELL. SO I HEARD, SO I SAW. . . .

"A hundred flowers fell" is a phrase from the poem "Untitled" by Li Shangyin (813–858). The Chinese poet was known for his "aestheticism" and left a number of "Untitled" poems.

Behind this sequence is John Ford's tragedy, *'Tis Pity She's a Whore.*

107 *Though he bragged, "I just was having a dream"*: The protagonist Kiyoaki's words at the end of *Spring Snow*, the first volume of Mishima Yukio's tetralogy.

108 *I have two daughters who have not known man*: From Genesis 19:7–8. *Laisse-moi, mon bien-aimé! laisse-moi partir!*: "Leave me, my beloved! Let me go!" From Paul Claudel's play *Le soulier de satin* (*The Satin Slipper*).

109 *Laisse-moi devenir une étoile!*: "Let me become a star!" Ibid. *O Marie, Reine du Ciel!*: "O Marie, Queen of Heaven!" Ibid. *Love that lasts for a moment turns to ashes in a moment*: From Li Shangyin's "Untitled." *And the Lord came down to see the city and the tower*: Genesis 11:5.

110 *nor a shining sea*: Allusion to Mishima Yukio's tetralogy *The Sea of Fertility*. *The twin big brother and kid sister*: Allusion to Richard Wagner's *Die Walküre* (*The Valkyrie*).

111 *et idcirco vocatum est nomen . . . eius Babel*: "That is why it was called Babel." From Genesis 11:9. *Something bitter as everyone knows?*: From Mishima Yukio's *The Sailor Who Fell from Grace with the Sea*, the fourth volume in his tetralogy.

BATHHOUSE

112 *Epigraphs*: Genesis 19: 27–28: "And Abraham gat up early in the morning to the place where he stood before the Lord: and he looked toward Sodom and Gomorrah, and toward all the land of the plain, and beheld, and, lo, the smoke of the country went up as the smoke of a furnace" (KJV). Dante: "After he turned back he seemed like one / who races for the green cloth on the plain / beyond Verona. And he looked more the winner / than the one who trails the field" (tr. by Robert and Jean Hollander).

113 *Ra-ri-re-ru*: Befuddled, potted by a drug. *I've given a modicum of money*: See Matthew 26:14–15. *Peter is said to have wept bitterly*: See Matthew 26:75.

115 *We are the hollow men*: From T. S. Eliot's "The Hollow Men." *The used tires are heavy. . .*: "Fred with Tires, Hollywood, 1984" in Herb Ritts's series of photos, *Bodyshop Series*. *O hole in the wall here!*: From Ezra Pound's "Marvoil." *gamboling sons are in other words the sons of God*: See John 1:12.

116   *On the ground skylarks . . .*: The word order of this verse in the original is upside down.

    in Lancashire four thousand holes: See the Beatles' song, "A Day in the Life."

117   *Nigra sum sed formosa*: "I *am* black, but comely, O ye daughters of Jerusalem, as the tents of Kedar, as the curtains of Solomon." Song of Solomon 1:5 (KJV).

    I ha' seen him eat o' the honey-comb: From Ezra Pound's "Ballad of the Goodly Fere." As Pound notes, "Simon Zelotes speaking after the Crucifixion. Fere = Mate, Companion."

    Sin' they nailed him to the tree: Ibid.

118   *Nod*: Puns with *nodo* in Japanese, "throat."

119   *Gloria Patri et Filio*: "Glory be to the Father and the Son." From the Lesser Doxology.

    And I Don't Say: AIDS acronym.

    Life is probably darker than death: Alludes to the refrain in "Das Trinklied vom Jammer der Erde" ("The Drinking Song of Earth's Misery")—the first movement of Gustav Mahler's orchestral song cycle, *Das Lied von der Erde* (*The Song of the Earth*).

120   *ego sum A et ω*: "I am the Alpha and the Omega." Revelation 1:8 (KJV).

    The pair of angels were (in truth): See Genesis 19:1–7.

    at once turn into salt: See Genesis 19:24–28.

121   *Or aspetta!*: "Now wait!" From Dante, *Inferno*, XVI:14.

    Bald, oder nie!: "Soon, or never!" From Mozart's *Die Zauberflöte* (*The Magic Flute*).

    Lacrimosa dies illa: "Tearful that day." From Mozart's *Requiem in D Minor*.

122   *What kind of bird is a cuckoo?*: One Japanese legend says that the cuckoo is the messenger of death. It echoes the Chinese legend that the soul of Emperor Shu turned into this bird.

    when Icarus fell / it was spring: From William Carlos Williams's poem "Pictures from Brueghel."

    Vae unum abiit: "One woe is past [*and,* behold, there come two woes more hereafter]." From Revelation 9:12.

    et abiit primus . . .: "And the first went, and poured out his vial upon the earth / and there fell a noisome and grievous sore upon the men which had the mark of the beast / and upon them which worshipped his image." Revelation 16:2 (KJV).

I shall be too late: The White Rabbit's first word in *Alice's Adventures in Wonderland*. Though this is often quoted, the expression was "I shall be late!" when the book was published.

A beast is slain, a beast thrives: From a line of Sir Geoffrey Hill's "Doctor Faustus."

123   *Being in this world is like a great dream!*: A line from Li Po's poem "On a Spring Day I Awake Drunken and Think." Hans Bethge adapted the poem in his translation, which Mahler used for *Das Lied von der Erde*.

"Ditto" said Tweedle . . .: From Lewis Carroll's *Through the Looking-Glass, and What Alice Found There*.

124   *Avoid all intercourse in the world*: From Dante's *Inferno*, XX: 85.

"I'm a Fawn!" it cried out: From Lewis Carroll's *Through the Looking-Glass*.

et efuge in Aegyptum: "and flee into Egypt." From the Vulgate, Gospel According to Matthew 2:13.

If you see kay / Tell him: In James Joyce's *Ulysses*, sung by The Prison Gate Girls.

125   *Still! Bub! Die Augen zu*: "Quiet! Boy! Close your eyes." From Alban Berg's opera *Wozzeck* that was based on Georg Büchner's play *Woyzeck*.

126   *et profugus in terra*: "a vagabond in the earth." Vulgate, Genesis 4:14 (KJV).

vox sanguinis fratris: "the voice of thy brother's blood." Vulgate, Genesis 4:10 (KJV).

"The mouth is a deep pit": From Proverbs 22:14.

127   *Schorach ani wenowach*: "I am black but comely." Transliterated Hebrew from James Joyce's *Ulysses*.

Qui vous a mis dans cette fichue position?: "Who put you in this wretched position?" Ibid.

C'était le sacré pigeon, Philippe: "It was the sacred pigeon, Philippe." Ibid.

non hunc sed Barabban: "not this man but Barabbas." Vulgate, John 18:40 (KJV).

ὡς δὲ καὶ ὀστέα . . .: "Therefore, let one single vessel, the golden two-handled / urn the lady your mother gave you, hold both our ashes" (tr. Richard Lattimore). The last part of Patroklos's ghost appearing to Achilleus in a dream.

128   Не рыдай Мене, Мати . . .: "Do not weep for me, Mother, when I
       am in my grave" (tr. Stanley Kunitz and Max Hayward). From Rus-
       sian poet Anna Akhmatova's "Requiem," section X ("Crucifixion").
       <mother's bone-colored milk>: From a haiku by Kamakura Sayumi.
       ecce mater tua: "behold your mother." Vulgate, Gospel According to
       John 19:27.
       kalaviṅka: The poet's mother's posthumous Buddhist name includes
       this fantastical bird with a human head and long tail from Buddhist
       mythology.

129   the other shore: From the Sanskrit word pāragate, the mantra in the
       short sutra Prajñā-pāramitā-hṛdaya, often translated as The Heart Sutra.
       Sunday at ten o'clock in the morning: See C. P. Cavafy's poem "Lovely
       White Flowers" (tr. Edmund Keeley and Philip Sherrard).
       गते (gah-teh): "Gone" in Sanskrit; often romanized as "gate." A word that
       appears in the last sentence of The Heart Sutra: "Gone, gone, everyone
       gone to the other shore, awakening, svaha."
       "The way is long, and difficult the road": "La via è lunga e 'l cammino
       è malvagio." From Dante's Inferno, Canto XXXIV, line 95 (tr. Henry
       Wadsworth Longfellow).

SAILING INTO THE LANDSCAPE
133   Handsome Sailor: From Herman Melville's Billy Budd, Sailor.
       Destined to stop a beer barrel: See Hamlet, Act V, scene 1: "Alexander
       died, Alexander was buried, / Alexander returneth into dust, the
       dust is earth, of earth we make loam, and why of that loam, whereto
       he was converted, might they not stop a beer-barrel?"

TATSUHIKO ISHII, poet and essayist, was born in Yokohama, Japan in 1952. For much of his life, he worked as a journalist for one of Japan's largest newspapers and book publishers, *The Asahi Shimbun*, covering cultural affairs locally and abroad, while also working for their editorial, advertising, and production departments. From the 1980s to the 1990s he was a theater critic for the weekly *Asahi Journal*. At age twenty he won the New Poet's Prize in Japan, and in 1997 he received an Asian Cultural Council grant to spend several months in the United States to research gay culture. Ishii has published a dozen collections of tanka since 1982, one edition of which appeared in France in 2012.

HIROAKI SATO is a translator of Japanese poetry and prose, classical and modern, who has won a PEN Translation Prize and two Japanese-U.S. Friendship Commission translation prizes. A newspaper and magazine columnist for forty years, particularly for *The Japan Times*, he also writes book reviews and essays for many publications. His nonfiction book *On Haiku* ("a treasure"—*Books on Asia*) and his translation of Sakutaro Hagiwara's *The Iceland* are both published by New Directions. He is also the author of the recent *A Bridge of Words: Views across America and Japan*.